A Place of Your Own

SIMON JAMES is a regular contributor to *Ideal Home* magazine. In 1980 he won the Argos Consumer Writer Award, having been a runner-up in the previous year.

SIMON JAMES

IDEAL HOME **A Place of Your Own**

How to preserve your sanity while setting up home

Illustrations by Honeysett

Hutchinson

London Melbourne Sydney Auckland Johannesburg

To Muriel, with whom I set up home

Hutchinson & Co. (Publishers) Ltd

An imprint of the Hutchinson Publishing Group

17-21 Conway Street, London W1P 6JD

Hutchinson Group (Australia) Pty Ltd
30-32 Cremorne Street, Richmond South, Victoria 3121
PO Box 151, Broadway, New South Wales 2007

Hutchinson Group (NZ) Ltd
32-34 View Road, PO Box 40-086, Glenfield, Auckland 10

Hutchinson Group (SA) (Pty) Ltd
PO Box 337, Bergvlei 2012, South Africa

First published 1982

© Simon James 1982

Illustrations © *Honeysett*

Typeset by V & M Graphics Ltd, Aylesbury, Bucks

Printed in Great Britain by the Anchor Press Ltd
and bound by Wm Brendon & Sons Ltd
both of Tiptree, Essex

ISBN 0 09 147901 0

Contents

Introduction ix

1 Choosing a Home 1
Types of home; deciding what you need; bedrooms; room to relax; the kitchen; the garage and garden; detached houses; semi-detached houses; terraced houses; bungalows; flats; maisonettes; new houses; mobile homes; self-built houses; making the choice

2 Renting a Home 14
The Housing Act 1980; furnished and unfurnished accommodation; shorthold tenancy; agreeing a fair rent; the landlord's agreement; a home with the job; the rent acts; co-ownership schemes; shared ownership schemes

3 Buying a Home: First Steps 22
Building societies; mortgage terms; types of mortgage; tax relief; deferred payment schemes; loans from insurance companies, local authorities and banks; matching the property to the loan; choosing where to live; dealing with estate agents; freehold or leasehold; estate agents' literature

4 Buying a Home: Taking a Look 35
Assessing the property; roofing faults; drainage systems; rising damp; dry rot and wet rot; settlement; damp and condensation; woodworm; wiring circuits; plumbing systems; making an offer; houses with vacant possession; bargaining; conservation areas

5 Buying a Recently-built House   49
The National House-Building Council; the Purchaser's Agreement; how to make a claim; the value of the guarantee

6 Buying a Home: Wheels in Motion   56
What a conveyancing solicitor does; the contract; solicitors' fees; the Homeloan scheme; engaging a surveyor; is your surveyor really necessary?; avoiding a contracts race; completion; cut-price conveyancing; conveyancing in Scotland

7 Moving in   68
Preparing the house; hiring a van; connecting supplies; redirecting mail; finding a doctor and a dentist

8 Peace of Mind   73
Buildings insurance; estimating rebuilding costs; contents insurance; assessing the value of the contents; insurance for tenants

9 Safe and Sound   81
Electrical fires; kitchen fires; inflammable furniture; inflammable decorating materials; tackling a fire; making the home secure against burglars; burglar alarms; falls in the home; electrical accidents; first aid

10 The Castle Syndrome   92
Authorized intruders; the rights of the police; bailiffs and sheriffs; valuation officers; your neighbours' rights; how to deal with trespassers and burglars; visitors' and tradesmens' rights

11 The Costs of Being a Householder   100
Rates; how rates are assessed; paying your rates; obtaining a rates reduction; budgeting for bills; direct debiting; crediting schemes; bank loans; gas tariffs; electricity tariffs; the price of solid fuel and oil

12 Improving Your Home 111
Central heating systems; storage heaters; insulating the home; double glazing; loft conversions; extensions; engaging an architect; finding a builder; building regulations; improvement and repair grants; modernizing a kitchen

13 Moving on: the Second Home 124
Leaving a rented home; whether or not to sell; having the house valued; selling through an estate agent; the contracts race; selling privately; how to word a newspaper advertisement; DIY conveyancing; showing prospective buyers your property; accepting an offer; selling property in Scotland

14 Moving out 134
Finding a removal firm; fixtures and fittings; removal estimates; packing; moving day

15 If Disaster Strikes Your Home . . . 141
What happens if you lose your home; your rights in law; who will help provide essentials

Appendix 144

Index 150

Introduction

'Seek home for rest, for home is best.'
　　　　　　　　　　　　THOMAS TUSSER (1524-80)

This book is for people setting up home for the first time: for buyers or renters, house- or flat-hunters, married or single, young or old – for all those who set out upon the exciting and challenging task of finding a place of their own. It is a task that should be enjoyed, but it can so easily turn sour through a hasty or ill-considered choice of dwelling, through high costs that might have been avoided, or through insufficient knowledge of the problems and responsibilities of being a householder or flatholder.

In this book I have attempted to smooth the way towards making the right choice – at the right price – and creating a comfortable and well-run home. The emphasis throughout is on saving – saving money, time and aggravation. Every effort has been made to ensure that the information given is accurate and up to date.

Few authors give public credit to their agent, but I would like to make an exception by thanking John Pawsey who first saw the need for a book such as this and encouraged me to write it. My thanks also to Terence Whelan, Editor of *Ideal Home* magazine, who enthused over the idea and suggested that the book should appear under the *Ideal Home* banner.

Many people and organizations provided help with the writing of this book: this ranged from professional advice to the experiences told to me by first-time homemakers – perhaps the best qualified to pronounce on the fortunes and misfortunes of setting up a home. I would like to mention in particular Gwyn Hughes, LL.B., Principal Lecturer in Law at the North London Polytechnic, who read all the sections of the book dealing with legal matters and made many useful suggestions. I am indebted also to John Field of the Housing Corporation, who kept me up to date with all aspects of co-ownership and shared ownership schemes. My thanks, too, to my wife Muriel, herself a journalist and Home Page Editor of a women's magazine, who helped with the research and professionally criticized the first draft. Some of the organizations that supplied information are included in the Appendix: all are willing to give further help to individual readers.

Last, but by no means least, my thanks to Andrew and Auriol, Chris and Catherine and Keith and Janette, three couples whose experiences I have faithfully chronicled in the hope that others may learn from them - as I did.

SIMON JAMES

1 Choosing a Home

'I know we plan to start a family, Brian, but don't you think we should start off with something a little smaller?'

Choosing a home is like buying a new pair of shoes – the style, quality and price are important, but the main needs are comfort and convenience. As with all things, buying a home must be done in the light of what you can afford, but it can be a mistake to let the cost be the overriding factor. It is all too easy to find a place that appears to be a bargain, only to discover after moving in that it is too small, badly designed or has other disadvantages that could have been avoided by choosing more carefully. When you buy shoes you usually try on several pairs, because once you have left the shop you cannot change your mind. Even more care should be taken over the choice of a home.

Comfort should therefore be the main aim. Decide what sort of home you will be comfortable in, and then look around to see what is available at the price you want to pay. The chances are that your dream home will cost more than you can afford; if so, you must lower your sights and settle for something less ambitious. But with patience and perseverance you will eventually arrive at a good compromise – a home at the right price and something near your ideal. Take your time about choosing, because time is on your side. As a first-time buyer you are free to pick and choose, to be fussy and hardheaded. It is an opportunity that cannot recur once you have become a home-owner.

Types of home

The range of homes is wide. Victorian middle-class families had large houses, standing behind laurels in secluded streets, but working-class folk had to be content with 'two up, two down' cottages standing shoulder to shoulder in Jubilee Terrace or Gasworks Lane. But fashions have changed, and many of those rambling old houses have now been converted into comfortable flats, while the humble cottages once thought of as near slums make ideal first buys for young couples with the time and enthusiasm to turn them into bright, cheerful homes.

It was not until after the First World War that home-ownership became a possibility for all, and the building trade was quick to oblige with homes to suit all tastes and pockets. Throughout the 1920s and '30s, detached and semi-detached houses and bungalows blossomed wherever land was available. In the towns, purpose-built flats and maisonettes sprang up either in blocks or above business premises.

After the Second World War, building concentrated mainly on council houses, but in the '50s houses for private sale began to appear in new styles and built according to new techniques. Today you are being wooed by property developers advertising 'Superhomes', 'Ideal Homes' and even 'Homes of the Future'.

Deciding what you need

Consider first of all your basic need - a comfortable home at a price you can afford. To be comfortable you need space, so you must determine how many rooms your home should have and the size they need to be. If you are a married couple planning an early family you will need as a minimum a lounge/dining room, kitchen, bathroom, w.c. and two bedrooms. That will be adequate for a number of years if you have only one child, and if both bedrooms are 'doubles' another addition to the family can be accommodated for several more years. After the age of about ten, however, children need their own rooms, especially if they are of different sexes.

Where there are no children, the extra bedroom will be useful for putting up guests, and even a third bedroom is worth considering. An extra room can fill many functions, such as a study, workshop, studio, photographic dark-room or even a gymnasium.

Bedrooms

Room sizes vary considerably; in some pre-war three-bedroomed houses the third 'bedroom' is little more than a box room and the architect apparently had midgets in mind when he designed the double bedroom. At least one good-size bedroom is essential - large enough to take a double or two single beds, bedside tables, a dressing-table, chest of drawers and one double or two single wardrobes. And all should fit easily with enough space to walk around the bed, open the

3

wardrobe doors and pull out drawers. Working couples, both of whom get dressed at the same time each morning, will find that a cramped bedroom can make for a very bad start to the day.

Remember, too, that your bedroom is the first thing you see when you wake up in the morning - a time when few of us are at our best - so you will want to see a room that is spacious and airy, without furniture that seems to crowd in on you.

Though occupied by only one person, a child's bedroom should be little smaller than its parents'. A cot, of course, does not take up much room, but before long a single bed or divan will be needed, as well as a bedside table and storage for clothes. There should also be enough space for the collection of dolls, train sets, model aeroplanes and cars that will mount up over the years. Ideally there should also be room for a bookcase and a desk and chair for doing homework. Looking even further ahead, consider also whether your child's bedroom will be large enough for entertaining friends. Not providing them with a room where they can talk and play pop records with their friends may be an oversight you will regret later.

Room to relax

After the kitchen, the most used room in your home will be the sitting room, living room or lounge. Here you will spend most of your leisure time - reading books, watching television, playing with the children, listening to your hi-fi or entertaining friends. Both the size and the shape of this room are important. It should be large enough for a three-piece suite (or equivalent), and perhaps a couple of occasional chairs, a television set, occasional table and possibly a sideboard or wall unit. The room's shape will very much determine where all these items should go, but avoid a room where, for instance, the settee will fit only in one place or only one wall is long enough for a wall unit. Give yourself the chance to move the furniture around from time to time. The shape of the room will also govern its character, and there are a number of features that can make a room pleasant and interesting. Alcoves at the sides of the chimney breast can be shelved to take books, houseplants or fine ornaments, and can be particularly pleasing if lit by concealed lighting. A bay window, apart from giving a little extra space, looks well with full-length curtains (but avoid covering radiators with curtains: they will take all the heat). Give some thought to picture rails: they are seldom found in new houses and many people remove them from old property, but they give a finishing touch to a wall if painted in a colour contrasting with the wallcovering. They can also be used for hanging pictures!

The kitchen

Pre-war, even the most modern kitchens were not designed for what were then considered luxuries, such as washing machines, refrigerators and dishwashers, but since then the kitchen, more than any other room in the house, has attracted the attention of interior designers and design consultants, and their ideas have transformed the often dingy and depressing sculleries of those days into bright, cheerful rooms which are a pleasure to work in. If you are going to buy an unmodernized pre-war house, be prepared for a kitchen that was designed to take the kitchen sink, a gas stove and little else. New houses, on the other hand, are likely to have architect-designed kitchens that will accommodate all the larger kitchen appliances in comfort.

Generally speaking, modern kitchen designs are of four main types: the single-line unit, in which all the work tops, appliances and cupboards are arranged along one wall; the galley assembly, with units on two long facing walls; the L-shape, with one section, usually the sink unit, at right angles to the other units; and the U-shape, which has units arranged on three sides of the kitchen. Your choice will be governed partly by personal taste, and very much by cost - the larger and better equipped the kitchen the more it will cost. But it is a room in which you are likely to spend a great deal of time, which is the work-centre of home and which all the family will use frequently, so its size and design are important. It may therefore be worth sacrificing some other item in order to have an efficient and comfortable kitchen.

Although there is often little difference between the price

of older houses and new ones of the same size, there are never enough new ones to go round. You may live in an area where there is little or no property being built owing to the shortage of building land. So you may have to buy older property with an existing kitchen that is poorly designed. Much can be done, however, to bring an old kitchen up to date: removing a chimney breast or extending the room to take in a disused coal-store or part of the garden will provide extra space; rearranging the plumbing and putting in extra power points will facilitate the use of modern appliances. Even if you cannot afford appliances such as dishwashers, washing machines and freezers when you first buy the house, it is worth making provision for them from the outset because re-plumbing and rewiring at a later date, when circumstances have changed and you *can* afford them, will be disruptive as well as more expensive.

These, then, are the main requirements for a comfortable home: good-size bedrooms, a large, pleasant lounge and an efficient, easy-to-run kitchen. The other rooms, though important for their particular function, are, after all, rooms of convenience. The dining room or area needs only to be large enough for a table, chairs and a sideboard. The bathroom needs no more space than that taken by the bath, wash-basin, bidet (if desired) and w.c., with enough room for, say, a mother to manipulate a large towel and a wet child, and some storage allowance. Remember that a very large bathroom will be difficult to heat.

The garage and garden

Outside the house you may want a garage, if the house does not already have one, but consider whether a carport or just a run-in to keep the car off the road would be sufficient. As for the garden, that is something you must decide for yourself. Even if you are a keen gardener, however, be careful not to take on something you have neither the time nor the money to keep in good order. And do not try to establish bowling-green lawns or beds of precious and delicate plants until the children have got past the scooter and go-cart age. Consider, instead, the more practical aspects, such as having enough space to stretch a decent length of clothes-line, a fence that will keep dogs out and children in, and a well-made garden path that will not turn into a muddy track in winter.

Detached houses

Most people consider a detached house their ideal; it offers privacy and the occupants will not be disturbed by noises coming through the party wall, nor will they cause such disturbance to their neighbours. They can hold wild parties, have the radio, hi-fi or television on at full blast or have a full-scale family row - all within reason, of course - without worrying about complaints from next door. Detached houses, however, are usually larger than other types with the same number of rooms, and they often have large gardens - and there's the rub, for that adds up to a high rateable value. How the rateable value is assessed and how rates are paid is dealt with in Chapter Eleven, but do you really want to pay extra for the privilege of total seclusion? If not, then the next best choice is a semi-detached house.

Semi-detached houses

The 'semi' has always been subjected to snobbery in the past, stemming from the days when builders and speculators strung them like beads along main roads or piled them together on housing estates. The houses are built in pairs, each being a 'mirror image' of its neighbour, and the result is row upon row of houses in which only the colour of the front door and curtains distinguishes one from another. Nevertheless, there are more semis than any other type of house in Britain, and thousands of families find them comfortable and convenient places in which to live.

The average good semi-detached house built pre-war usually has a kitchen or kitchenette, sitting room or lounge, dining room, bathroom and w.c. and three bedrooms. The garden may be a modest plot at the front, with enough room for a small lawn, flower beds and vegetable garden at the rear. There may be a garage or parking space at the side of the house. The rateable value should be reasonable.

The only real disadvantage of a semi is that party wall, the one that divides your house from your neighbour's. In many pre-war houses, and unfortunately in some modern ones, this wall is pretty thin. But the problem of noise can be overcome by fitting sound-proof panelling in one or all of the rooms.

Terraced houses

If the semi has suffered from snobbery, it has got off lightly compared with the contempt heaped upon terraced houses and cottages. Many were built in Victorian and Edwardian times in long rows, often with no individual side or rear access. They are often rather small, with two rooms upstairs and two rooms down; some have a front door opening directly from the pavement into the front room, an outside toilet and a scullery rather than a kitchen.

But although they were cheap to build they have stout walls, strong timber floors and well slated roofs. They lend themselves well to modification and improvement, which can often be carried out with a local authority grant. Possible improvements might include adding an extension to make a large kitchen or enlarge the existing one, fitting a Georgian-style bow-window at the front; removing the centre wall to make one large downstairs room and modifying the outside w.c. to give access from inside the house; or sacrificing the smallest bedroom to make a proper bathroom with its own w.c. Many of these changes have already been made by young first-time buyers and such property is well worth looking out for. Unfortunately, once a whole street of such houses has been modernized the area will be pronounced 'fashionable' and the prices will suddenly rise.

Sharing two walls with your neighbours is usually less of a disadvantage in terraced houses than in semis, because of the thickness of the walls. And with only two outside walls the house is easier and cheaper to keep warm. The only real disadvantage is the lack of space, even with modifications, and of course your car will have to stand in the road unless you can rent a nearby lock-up garage. But terraced houses undoubtedly provide a sound first-rung-of-the-ladder buy for young couples and are also a good buy for single people.

Bungalows

Among the most sought-after properties are bungalows, but because of the amount of ground they occupy they are always more costly to buy than houses with similar room space. The bungalow craze started in the 1920s, but they became less popular with builders when building land became scarce. They are available detached or semi-detached, and their main advantage is that they have no stairs, which is a boon for older people and also allows more space for the rooms.

A medium-size bungalow usually has a large sitting room or lounge, two good-size bedrooms, a bathroom, probably with a separate w.c., and a kitchen. If you want a third or fourth bedroom then you will need either a large-size bungalow or one that has had an extension added – and the rateable value will be very high. Bungalows are not ideal for large families, or people contemplating having a large family, because of the small number of rooms. They are more suitable for childless couples or people whose children have grown up and left home.

Flats

Many single people start off in a flat when they leave home, and a large proportion of couples also opt for a flat when they start married life together. Since the war many of the old Victorian houses, often three storeys tall, have been converted to a high standard of comfort, with two rooms, bathroom and kitchen taking up all of one floor. Sometimes there are separate entrances, which make the flats completely self-contained. This type of flat, however, is almost always rented. Few building societies will consider a loan for buying a converted flat unless the conversion is of an exceptionally high standard.

Purpose-built flats can seldom be bought freehold; they are usually sold on a long lease with the tenant paying a ground rent and perhaps a share of the cleaning and maintenance costs of stairs and passageways. Building societies usually require at least thirty years of the lease to be remaining when making a loan.

Maisonettes

Maisonettes are two-storey flats, often built in blocks of four or six or above a parade of shops. There are no shared passageways and each unit has its own front door. They can be bought leasehold in the same way as purpose-built flats, and are an attractive first buy for working couples who do not intend to start a family for some years to come. They are not, however, easy to come by, particularly outside the larger towns.

New houses

Builders and property-developers put a great deal of effort, and money, into persuading people to buy new houses. Some even claim to guarantee a mortgage. It has to be admitted that buying brand-new property – a home where everything is new and where no one has lived before – can be an attractive proposition. One disadvantage, however, is that a new house has to be 'run in', like a new car. A new house contains about 1,000 gallons of water in its structure, and that means condensation problems as the house dries out (not a good thing if there is a young baby around). You cannot paint or paper the walls for at least six months, and cracks caused by natural settlement may go on appearing for years. Other faults may occur, which a good builder will put right as soon as possible, but they can still be inconvenient. Often the best bet is to buy a house that is about five years old; it will have been 'run-in' and most of its problems will have been sorted out.

If you decide to buy a new house, you can do so even before it is built by putting down a deposit with a builder and selecting something from his range. But architect's plans can be deceptive to the inexperienced eye and the finished house may turn out to be rather different from what you expected. Ask the builder to let you see an example of the type of house you wish to buy; he may have 'show homes' on his site but failing that he should be able to arrange for you to visit a house that he has recently sold.

This will also give you the chance to talk to the owners, who will quickly point out any design snags that are not apparent before moving in. If the builder is reluctant to let you see one of his houses, view him with suspicion: no one should be expected to buy anything purely on paper, let alone a house costing many thousands of pounds.

The range of new houses include detached, semi-detached, bungalows and even terraced houses, though the modern term for these is 'town houses'. Some builders specialize in purpose-built town houses for single people, and several offer special help for first-time buyers, such as low-deposit mortgages and deferred-payment loans.

The standard of new houses is generally higher than in pre-war houses, brought about by stricter building regulations and by the actions of the National House-Building Council.

Mobile homes

A type of dwelling that has been introduced comparatively recently is the 'mobile home', a term usually associated with caravans and houseboats. But the latest in mobile homes is a factory-built unit which can be taken by road to a specially prepared site. These homes are built to high standards using the latest materials and technology, according to British Standard (BS) 3632.

Each home is complete, right down to furniture, curtains and carpets, and once on site all that needs to be done is to 'plug-in' to the main services – water, gas and electricity. The units are bungalows, available with one, two or three bedrooms, and prices are well below those of a conventionally-built dwelling. Hire purchase terms are available.

Mobile home companies claim that the value of these homes increases in the same way as conventional houses, but there is one snag in selling a mobile home: it must first be offered to the company from whom it was bought. Nevertheless such homes are worth considering as a first buy, especially for single people and young working couples. Their mobility is an advantage if you should need to move to another part of the country, for example, to change jobs, because you can take your home with you, providing there is a site in that area.

The homes can be seen at show sites, or you can select one from one of the company's detailed brochures.

Self-build houses

There is one other alternative available if you want a new house: you can build it yourself. But you will need plenty of spare time, plus the will to see the project through. It is best to join, or help form, a self-build group, and there are self-build management firms who will give technical advice on building and on buying the land. They will charge a fee, of course, but this usually works out at about £20 to £30 for a group of ten people. The National Federation of Housing Associations (see Appendix) will supply names of reputable self-build management firms.

Making the choice

That then, is the wide choice of homes available to you as a first-time buyer. Now you must make up your mind which appeals to you most before you set out on your search. But before doing so, take a look at what three young couples chose recently, and as you read through the next few chapters you will see how they fared and learn something from their fortunes and misfortunes. Their names are Andrew and Auriol, Chris and Catherine and Keith and Janette, and all were able to buy their first home under £20,000.

First, Andrew and Auriol: they opted for an Edwardian terraced house in a street where many young people had already shown what can be done with that type of property. They hope to do the same and are already modernizing the kitchen. They have set aside the small third bedroom as a studio where they can both paint. Chris and Catherine also chose a terraced house, and were lucky enough to find one of rather unusual design. Built pre-war, it has a Georgian-style bow window at the front, looking out to a small garden and a tree-lined road. An attractive hallway leads through to a small kitchen, a dining room with french windows and a conservatory. Upstairs there are three bedrooms and a modern bathroom.

Keith and Janette's house is also pre-war and terraced. In their case they bought from a young couple who had themselves been first-time buyers three years ago. Though smaller than the houses bought by the other two couples, it has a large, fully-fitted kitchen and has been redecorated throughout. All the windows have been replaced by modern aluminium-frame units, double-glazed, and all carpets and curtains were included in the sale. Keith and Janette are at work all day and have no plans for starting a family, so the two bedrooms, lounge and kitchen are just right for them.

Those three couples have one other thing in common: they chose carefully, turning down anything that did not quite appeal to them, however attractively priced. But each has a story or two to tell of their experiences once they had said to the estate agent, 'We like it'.

2 Renting a Home

'And if this landlord doesn't believe he's your brother we'll be evicted for keeping pets again.'

Most people seeking a home want eventually to own it, and the arguments in favour of home-ownership as against renting accommodation are undeniably strong. Buying a home is an investment, whereas renting a home means paying week after week for something you will never own. Home-ownership gives you independence, but in rented property you must abide by rules laid down by the landlord. In your own home you are totally secure, but as a tenant you can be evicted.

Nevertheless, home-ownership is beyond the reach of many people. As house prices rise faster than incomes it becomes more and more difficult to save enough money to put down a deposit, and for low wage earners there is little chance of getting a mortgage. Renting a home is the only alternative, but apart from the disadvantage of never owning the property there is no reason why anyone should not become a tenant and at the same time enjoy much of the freedom and security enjoyed by home-owners.

Accommodation for rent is much harder to come by than property for sale. Less than half of the homes in Britain are rented, and more than one-third of those are owned by local authorities (as 'council houses').

The Housing Act 1980

Housing authorities in Britain include local councils, New Town Development Corporations, The Commission for New Towns and the Development Board for Rural Wales. All are subject to the Housing Act 1980 (as also are housing associations, trusts and co-operatives), which gives a number of legal rights to 'secure tenants'. A secure tenant is anyone whose house or flat is self-contained and is their only or principal home.

The most important provision of the Act, sometimes called the 'Tenants' Charter', is that a secure tenant cannot be evicted unless the landlord obtains a court order for re-possession. And to obtain such an order he must satisfy the court that there is good reason for wanting re-possession. The reason may be failure to pay rent, causing a nuisance to neighbours, damaging the property or obtaining a tenancy by making a false statement. In some cases, for example, if he wants to demolish the property in order to improve the site, if the dwelling is overcrowded, or if it was intended for people with a special need (e.g. disabled persons) and such persons no longer live there, the landlord can re-possess but must also provide suitable alternative accommodation.

The decision as to what is 'suitable' accommodation is made by the court, and will include consideration of the location as well as the dwelling itself.

Other rights now given to housing authority tenants include the freedom to make substantial improvements to the property, which will sometimes be eligible for a Home Improvement Grant on the same basis as privately owned property, and such improvements will not affect the rent. The Tenants' Charter also includes the controversial 'right to buy'; this has been a bone of contention between Tory and Labour governments and as such should not be regarded as a permanent feature of the Act.

Unfortunately, local authority accommodation is very scarce. After the Second World War, thousands of council houses were built but this supply has now dwindled to a trickle and in some areas has ceased altogether. Consequently the waiting lists have become longer and longer. Different councils operate different schemes for selecting tenants, the most common being the points system. Points may be given on the grounds of ill-health or overcrowding; in some areas points are given to people who were born in the area or have lived there most of their lives. Points are also given for each child of a family, and in many areas it is impossible for a childless couple to get on the waiting list.

Furnished and unfurnished accommodation

So the best that most home-seekers can hope for is privately rented accommodation, and here, too, there are new laws protecting tenants. At one time there was a vast difference between renting furnished and unfurnished property, tenants of unfurnished accommodation enjoying more security than those in furnished dwellings. Now the same rights apply to all. Like the council tenant, the private tenant cannot be evicted as long as he pays his rent and abides by the landlord's rules. Otherwise the landlord can only move him out if he wants to occupy the dwelling himself, or if the tenant has signed a 'shorthold tenancy' agreement.

Shorthold tenancy

A shorthold tenancy agreement guarantees the tenant the right to stay in his home for a specified period, anything from one to five years. He can leave at any time during that period after giving notice – one month for up to two-year tenancies and three months for three – to five-year tenancies. The landlord must give him three months' notice at the end of the agreed tenancy; he cannot give the tenant notice to leave before the expiry of the specified period of the tenancy.

Agreeing a fair rent

Rent is agreed by the landlord with the tenant, but if the tenant thinks it is too high he can seek a reduction through the local rent officer. If the rent officer sets a fair rent the landlord canot raise it for two years. If the tenant pays rent weekly he should ask for a rent book. This is his right by law, and it should contain the address of the premises; the name and address of the landlord; the amount of rent, stating whether it includes or excludes rates; the amount of rates payable and whether the rent has been fixed by law.

It is illegal for a landlord to demand rent in advance for unfurnished property, or to charge a premium, i.e. key money.

It is not necessary to have a rent book if the rent is paid less frequently than weekly, say monthly or quarterly, but it is a good idea to have one as there will then be a record of payments should there be any dispute.

The landlord's agreement

In addition to agreeing the rent, the tenant will almost certainly be required to sign an agreement specifying what he can and cannot do in his home. This is the landlord's 'rule book' and should be studied very carefully. 'No children' is one very common rule; 'no pets' is another, though this usually applies to cats and dogs and is unlikely to affect goldfish, but it may apply to caged birds so check with the landlord. Naturally the landlord will not agree to the tenant making any major changes to the property, such as knocking down a wall, but he may allow him to put up shelves and hang pictures. If you are thinking of renting private accommodation, check first exactly what the rules will and will not allow.

Entertaining guests is another matter you should clarify: few landlords would object to you having friends in for an evening, but there may be a rule against them staying the night or for a number of nights, especially if you are living in a small flat. The landlord may also insist on the right to enter your home from time to time in order to inspect the premises, but he can only do so with your permission and he has no right to hold a duplicate key. He has the right to be given access in order to carry out repairs, but again he must choose a reasonable time to do so.

An agreement for furnished property will usually include an inventory of furniture. This works in your interest, because you cannot later be accused of removing items that were not there in the first place. But check the condition of the furnishings and insist on any faults such as 'chair with broken leg' being noted on the inventory. Cigarette burns on tables and carpets are a common cause of dispute. You may find that the landlord has entered the value of each piece on the inventory - if so, beware, especially if the values are obviously inflated. In furnished accommodation a substantial proportion of the rent is for the hire of the furniture, and by listing high values the landlord will be trying to justify a high rent. You can strike out the values before signing the agreement, but more than likely the landlord will then refuse to rent you the property - and you will be better off without it!

What constitutes furnished property? In the case of dispute a county court can decide, but you are entitled to expect each room to be adequately furnished with the appropriate furniture, e.g., a bed, wardrobe and dressing-table in the bedroom. A court will assess the value of the property to the tenant without regard to its monetary value: for example, it would consider a bed to be of more value than a Chippendale cabinet.

A home with the job

There is one other type of rented accommodation to be considered, and that is the home that goes with a job.

People who are given accommodation so that they can carry out their work efficiently, for example, caretakers, servants and teachers in boarding schools, are not considered tenants in law. Their rent is fixed by their employer and the courts cannot intervene. Employee-tenants must leave the accommodation when their employment ceases. Such people are obviously very vulnerable, but they are in good company – the occupant of No. 10 Downing Street has no more rights to that property than the caretaker of a block of flats has to his!

An employee provided with housing as a fringe benefit, however, has the full protection of the law – whatever type of accommodation he occupies.

The Rent Acts

All rented accommodation is subject to the Landlord and Tenant Law, generally known as the Rent Acts, and over the years as the legislation has been changed or added to, the law has become more and more complex. We have looked at some aspects, but if you have any doubts about your rights you should consult a solicitor or get advice from the Citizens'. Advice Bureau.

Co-ownership schemes

There is one way of getting a home in which you become both a tenant and joint owner – by joining a co-ownership society. Co-ownership housing is planned and developed by non-profit-making housing associations and societies, using loans from building societies or the Housing Corporation. The residents take responsibility for both mortgages and management through an elected committee who are responsible to the co-owners for their affairs and the running of the estate, e.g. a block of flats or a group of houses.

Anyone over the age of eighteen can apply for membership and accommodation in a co-ownership scheme, but he must first satisfy the committee that he can pay his way and will get on well with his fellow members. To become a member you buy a non-returnable £5 share and sign a tenancy agreement which lays down your rights and responsibilities and specifies your monthly costs.

The monthly charge for your dwelling is linked to the value of the property at the time you move in and the cost of its upkeep. One month's rent is payable in advance, together with a returnable cash deposit usually equivalent to three months' rent. This is held by the society to cover any repairs or redecorating necessary when you leave.

It is when you leave that the main advantage of a co-ownership scheme operates, for then you receive a premium payment. This is based on a percentage of the increase in value of the property and also credits you with the amount you have paid towards the mortgage repayment. For example, if you occupy a flat that was worth £12,500 when you moved in and the value has risen to £18,750 when you leave, your premium, assuming a percentage payment of 56 per cent, could be £3,500. No payment is made until a new co-owner is found to take your place, and you are entitled to the premium only if you have occupied the dwelling for at least five years.

Under the 1980 Housing Act the 'right to buy' applies to co-ownership schemes, so that this type of rented property is becoming difficult to obtain as flats and houses are bought by the tenants.

Shared ownership schemes

A more recent scheme, proposed by the Housing Corporation and taken up by several housing associations, is shared ownership. This involves 'staircasing', by which the tenant can progressively increase his share of the property until he owns it outright. The Housing Corporation's proposal is that a tenant should start with a 25 per cent share and increase it to 100 per cent in 25 per cent steps, but individual associations can vary the scheme to suit their members.

The aims of housing associations are to help people who find that initial deposit for a mortgage just a bit too much for them. New ways of setting people on the road to home-ownership are constantly being devised, and it is well worth finding which housing associations are operating in the area in which you wish to live. For full information on housing associations you should get in touch with the National Federation of Housing Associations or the Housing Corporation (see Appendix).

3 Buying a Home: First Steps

'*I'm beginning to wish we hadn't left our name with quite so many estate agents.*'

Few people are fortunate enough to be able to pay cash for a house, so the large majority have to take out a mortgage. The literal meaning of the word mortgage, incidentally, is 'death pledge', and it dates from the days when the heir to a title, or property, could borrow money against the time when he would come into his inheritance on his father's death. Nowadays you simply pledge your property as security against the loan with which the property is bought - and that loan can come from a building society, bank, assurance company or local authority.

Building societies

Building societies have existed for more than 200 years, and were legally recognized in 1812. They are constituted under Acts of Parliament which define their functions and the way they must be managed. The law ensures that the societies are run in such a way as to minimize the risk of loss both to investors or borrowers.

Basically, building societies have two functions: they offer savings accounts for investors and they provide loans for the purpose of house purchase.

The money for the loans comes from the savings accounts. To attract investors the building societies offer good rates of interest, which at one time were better than those offered by banks. Recently, however, some of the High Street banks have increased the interest they pay on deposit accounts in an attempt to win more investors.

You do not have to save with a building society to become a borrower, but it sometimes helps when the society's funds are low because they then give priority to investors. Making regular investments also shows that you are a thrifty person capable of making loan repayments. It is wise, therefore, to start saving with a building society long before you are ready to ask for a mortgage: the more you have invested the better are your chances of getting a loan quickly. First-time buyers can also benefit from the government's Homeloan scheme (see page 62).

The choice of building societies is wide, and they all compete fiercely for business, as anyone who reads the newspapers or watches commercial television will know. But whether you want to be 'with the Woolwich' or 'get a little extra help' from the Halifax depends on what they will offer you when the time comes to ask for a loan.

Mortgage terms

Mortgage terms differ from society to society, so shop around carefully and study the leaflets available from local branch offices. You may find, for example, that one society will give you a mortgage after you have been saving with them for only six months; another may insist on you saving with them for at least twelve months. You should also keep in mind what type of property you wish to buy; some societies are loath to lend money on old property and some are not too keen on flats. If the leaflets do not tell you what you want to know, ask at the office.

You may also find slight variations in the amount you can borrow – always a percentage of the valuation price of the property. This also varies depending on the state of the society's finances. Generally you should have no difficulty in getting an 80 per cent loan on property up to the value of £25,000, depending of course on your salary (see below); above that the percentage may be only 75 per cent, or even 65 per cent on property valued at more than £40,000. The interest, too, may be higher on more expensive property.

Often the percentage of the loan is increased if you take out a mortgage guarantee policy (see Chapter Eight) which covers both you and the building society should you fall on hard times. Some societies insist on this insurance for first-time buyers, but will lend 95 per cent or even 100 per cent.

All building societies' rules regarding the amount they will lend and the length of time you are required to be an investor depend on the availability of funds. So you could start saving with one society with the hopes of obtaining an 85 per cent mortgage after six months, only to find later that the rules have changed and you can get only an 80 per cent loan after twelve months or more. That, unfortunately, is an unavoidable risk, but it can be offset by saving with more than one society.

When you approach your local building society manager you will have to convince him that you will be able to repay the loan. Most building societies will be prepared to lend you up to the equivalent of two and a half times your annual salary, and will take into account your spouse's earnings in full, assuming that is the lower salary. Thus if you are earning £8,000 p.a. they will lend you £20,000, and if in addition your spouse earns £3,000 p.a. the loan would be £23,000. With an 85 per cent mortgage that means you could buy a house at around £27,000, with a deposit of £4,000 to find.

But avoid stretching yourself to the limit on mortgage repayments. You may eventually start a family, in which case the mother's earnings will cease for a number of years. Also the interest on your repayments may fluctuate with the general rate of interest and the tendency is for interest rates to go up much quicker than they come down! In the example given above it would be prudent to go for property in the £25,000 bracket and avoid that well-worn but all-too-true cliché, a millstone around your neck. You will also need some cash in hand when you start to negotiate a purchase, as you will see later in the book.

Types of mortgage

Building societies offer two types of mortgage: the repayment mortgage and the endowment mortgage. With the repayment mortgage you repay the loan over a specified period of years (generally not more than twenty-five) and repayments are made in equal monthly instalments. If the interest rate changes your repayments are recalculated so that the loan is paid off over the agreed period. In the early years of a mortgage, the major part of your instalments goes to paying off the interest, but as the amount of the outstanding mortgage reduces the proportion of interest reduces also, and the repayment of the actual loan increases.

With an endowment mortgage, you make monthly payments consisting of the interest only, and take out an endowment policy with an assurance company which then pays off the loan when the policy matures, or on your earlier death. There are several types of endowment policy: you can have a non-profit endowment which simply provides a sum equal to the amount of your loan, or you can have a with-profit endowment which pays off the loan and also provides you with a bonus when the policy matures. There are also low-cost endowments which combine a with-profits policy with a mortgage protection policy. The bonus on this type of policy is not guaranteed, but there is usually a small lump sum payable to you after you have finished paying off the mortgage.

Both repayment and endowment mortgages are available under the Option Mortgage Scheme: this scheme was introduced by the government to help people who do not pay enough income tax to qualify for tax relief on mortgage interest. The scheme gives you the opportunity to forgo tax relief in return for a government subsidy which is paid to the building society, and which therefore reduces your monthly payments.

Deciding which type of mortgage will suit you best can be very confusing, and there are advantages and disadvantages in both repayment and endowment mortgages. In the long run an endowment mortgage is the more expensive of the two, but it can benefit the high tax-payer because the monthly payments consist entirely of the interest. So tax relief is given throughout the period of the loan. The amount of interest paid on a repayment mortgage reduces over the years until eventually the monthly instalments consist of repaying the loan itself, and therefore tax relief ceases.

On the other hand, however, a repayment mortgage is more flexible because the term can be extended beyond the original agreed period if there is a sharp rise in interest rates or if you fall on hard times. Or you can opt to pay the interest only for a period. Because an endowment mortgage pays only the interest to the mortgagee, over a period fixed by the terms of the insurance policy, you have no choice other than to pay the increased rate. (The terms 'mortgagor' and 'mortgagee' can be confusing: because a mortgage is a pledge, the mortgagor is the person making the pledge, i.e. the home-buyer, and the mortgagee is the party accepting the pledge, namely the bank or building society.) Another disadvantage of endowment mortgages may arise in later years when you want to move. You may need a fresh mortgage for your next house, and if you want to take out another endowment mortgage you will find the insurance premiums will be higher because of your increased age. So for first-time buyers paying the basic rate of tax, the repayment mortgage is the best choice, and has the advantage that repayments after tax relief are lower in the early years.

Tax relief

Tax relief is given on the total amount of interest you pay yearly – the amount is deducted from your income before tax is calculated. Therefore, if your mortgage repayments are £600 per year and £550 of that is interest, then £550 of your income is tax free. Your tax relief relates to the rate you pay, in other words if you pay tax at 30 per cent then you are allowed 30p in each £1 of interest, so you pay only 70p. At a tax level of 40 per cent you get a tax relief of 40p in the £1. If you pay tax under Schedule D, you must apply for the tax relief on the mortgage interest paid during the previous year when you do your tax returns (on tax form 11). Give the name and address of the mortgagee and your account or roll number. Note that full tax relief is given only on loans of up to £25,000. On loans in excess of that amount the tax relief is on the first £25,000 only.

The way tax relief is deducted at the moment applies only until April 1983, when the government will be introducing a new method designed to save administrative costs. The amount of tax relief will remain the same, but will be deducted from the mortgage repayments by the lender instead of from the house-buyer's PAYE tax. For example, a person with an £8,000 mortgage (at a mortgage rate of 15 per cent) pays £103.20 a month and claims tax relief against PAYE. From April 1983 the monthly repayments will fall to £73.20 and the relief on income will be abolished. Overall, people who have been repaying a mortgage for some time will end up paying the same as before, but new borrowers will be at a distinct disadvantage. This is because under the present scheme the major part of the mortgage repayments goes towards paying off the interest, as explained above, but under the new scheme it will be assumed that each instalment will consist of half interest and half repayment of the original capital borrowed. Therefore, the monthly tax relief, given only on the interest, will be lower for new mortgages.

While still on the subject of mortgage repayments, let us refer back for a moment to that constant worry of all mortgagors – what to do when the interest rates go up. For many people with repayment mortgages there is a strong temptation to offset the increase by extending the loan term.

Unless there is no alternative, the temptation should be avoided because it means that the overall cost of the house purchase increases in the long term. It is better either to meet the increased payments, or to arrange to pay the interest only until the rate falls again. Alternatively, if you are a taxpayer you can benefit by switching to an option mortgage (see page 26).

Deferred payment schemes

There is one other type of mortgage operated by some societies and by at least one large firm of builders. This is the Deferred Payment Mortgage Scheme, aimed at first-time buyers who have low incomes and wish to purchase a low-cost home. With this scheme you pay approximately 20 per cent less in the first year than you would with an ordinary repayment mortgage. The amount you pay rises each year until the fifth year, when you start paying what you would have paid in the first year of a repayment mortgage. For the next five years you pay the same as you would with a repayment mortgage, and from the eleventh year to the end of the term you pay more. Thus the large payments are 'deferred' until such time as your income has risen. This type of mortgage is therefore ideal for people with good career prospects. It is also available as an option mortgage (page 26).

Loans from life assurance companies, local authorities and banks

Three other loan sources are local authorities, life assurance companies and banks. Local authorities, because the government restricts the amount they can lend, tend to grant loans mainly on older property. They will sometimes offer a loan on a property that a building society has refused; in fact, some authorities will consider a loan only under those circumstances. There is usually a limit to what they will lend, but they are far more likely to give a 100 per cent loan than a building society. All types of mortgage are available from local authorities, including deferred payment schemes.

Getting a mortgage from an assurance company will almost always involve taking out a life assurance policy, which is in any case not a bad thing. A few companies combine life assurance with a guarantee of a mortgage after you have been paying the premiums for at least three years. This is a useful scheme for engaged couples who do not intend to get married for a number of years, and if you are under the age of thirty the premiums for a life assurance are low. As with an endowment mortgage, the assurance company pays off the loan from the life assurance policy, but one snag with this scheme is that you are unlikely to know what size mortgage you will want three years ahead.

You may get an endowment mortgage from an assurance company, but usually only on more expensive property. This method works in the same way as a combined endowment policy/building society mortgage except that the money is borrowed direct from the assurance company. The rate of interest on the loan is usually fixed, an advantage if you take out a loan at a time when interest rates are low.

Endowment mortgages have come in for some criticism, since insurance brokers and agents eager to get their commission have tended to give examples of how money can be saved by basing their calculations for tax relief on the average for the whole term, thereby overlooking inflation. Nevertheless, endowment mortgages can benefit the high wage-earner, though perhaps not so much as it would at first appear, and young people can benefit from the low cost of insurance.

Banks have only recently entered into the home loan market, and are competing with the building societies in this field as well as trying to attract savers. Bank loans for house purchase are made on much the same terms as building society mortgages - two and a half times the borrower's income with the spouse's earnings taken into account. Loans 80-90 per cent of the purchase price can be had, and the interest on the loan compares favourably with that charged by building societies.

One advantage of borrowing from a bank is that your request for a loan will not be turned down for lack of funds, as can happen with a building society.

Matching the property to the loan

Once you have satisfied yourself that a loan will be available you can start looking at property, and now is the time when the two factors governing your choice, what you want and what you can afford, come together. What you will be looking for in your search for a home is how to blend the two in the best possible way.

Try to stay within your price range and do not be tempted to go for something that is 'only another £500', especially if this will take you into a higher Stamp Duty bracket (see Chapter Six). That is not to say that you should not look at property advertised slightly above your price, because most house vendors ask for more than they expect to get.

The three first-time buyers introduced in Chapter One all obtained mortgages from building societies, and in Andrew and Auriol's case they bought a house that had been repossessed by a building society, which was anxious to re-sell the property and was therefore willing to offer a mortgage. Keith and Janette came a little unstuck with their loan, because the price they were paying for the house included the carpets and curtains and the building society's surveyor did not include these in his valuation. This is a point worth remembering: if you buy a house including fittings of any kind, the building society will exclude them and you may find that your mortgage is based on a price several hundred pounds lower than the price you are paying.

Chris and Catherine took the mortgage hurdle successfully and were helped by the fact that the estate agent was also an agent for a building society, so the loan went through fairly quickly. Catherine, a trainee journalist, was also able to persuade the building society to take into account a salary rise due several months ahead.

Notice that in these three cases the couples all found what they wanted first and applied for a mortgage afterwards, but they all agree this could have been a mistake. They were lucky, because they bought at a time when mortgages were fairly easy to get, but they realize now that they could have come unstuck and lost the homes they had set their hearts on if mortgages had not been readily available.

Choosing where to live

Your choice of area will obviously be governed very much by

personal taste: you may want to be near friends and relatives or simply want to stay where you have lived happily for many years. But the biggest single factor in deciding where to live will be its distance from where you work. You will need to know travelling times and, more important, the cost of travel, since you must budget for this, and future fare increases, when you come to assess your outgoings as a householder.

If you intend to travel by rail, find out the cost of a season ticket and whether you can get an interest-free loan for it from your employer. And if you will be driving to the station, check on parking facilities: British Rail car parks can be quite expensive and the fees usually rise at the same time as an increase in fares. Check, too, on bus services from where you live to the station. It may be cheaper to travel by bus, and a good service will be handy if for any reason you cannot use your car.

Needless to say, petrol prices must be considered if you intend driving to work, but you should also check on your route: are there traffic hold-ups along the way at peak hours?

These considerations apply particularly if you decide to live in a rural area, and there are many temptations to do so. Property in outlying districts is generally cheaper than in towns, and many builders and developers are offering homes built on estates in the country. Fresh, fine views over rolling countryside and a lovely old village pub just down the road – these are strong enticements. But what is it like in winter, when snow-blocked lanes keep the postman and milkman out and you in? And is there a good bus service to the nearest town, or do they run every two hours with the last one going through about tea-time?

If you decide to live out of town, then you will certainly need a car, and possibly two if your spouse works in a different area. On top of all that there are local amenities to take into account, such as shops, schools, library, banks and a post office, not to mention social considerations such as restaurants, theatres and cinemas. If you are determined to live in the country, then either the inconveniences or the costs of overcoming them must be borne, but if you are accustomed to town life then perhaps you will find the concrete jungle preferable to fresh fields and pastures new.

Dealing with estate agents

Unless you are buying a new house direct from a builder, the best way to start looking for what you want is through an estate agent. Estate agents sell houses for clients, who pay a commission when the house is sold. There is no charge to anyone buying a house through an agent. You will have no difficulty in finding them in any town, for during the last ten years or so they have blossomed in every High Street along with blue-jeans shops and Chinese take-aways. They fall into two classes: the older-established firms in Georgian premises with pinstripe-suited gentlemen who offer you a seat as soon as you walk in, and the newer concerns with revolving ads in the window, MGBs and TR7s outside the door and handsome young salesmen reeking of after-shave and sitting behind imitation teak desks. They all have one thing in common: they are in business to sell houses. All are capable of bending the Trades Descriptions Act to its limits, and their literature is sometimes as fanciful and highly-coloured as Walt Disney cartoons.

All this is to warn you that in house-buying the old principle of *caveat emptor* (let the buyer beware) holds good. Once you have bought a house you cannot take it back and change it.

On your first visit to an estate agent you may well find that he has several properties within your price range to offer you. In addition, you will be bombarded with leaflets about properties that are totally unsuitable, despite your careful description of what you want.

These will be properties he has had on his books for months, and having recognized you as a beginner in the house-hunting game he will be hoping you might just be naive enough to fall for a quick sale. Take the leaflets and move on to the next agent after leaving your name and address. When you have been to all the agents in the area, sit down and go through the leaflets.

The leaflet may include a photograph of the house, which will help you decide whether to read on or not, then there will be a short description of the property telling you when it was built, where it is and any other selling points such as whether it has central heating, double-glazing, etc.

Then follows a room-by-room description of the house, giving the size of each room and any features such as power points, radiators, fireplaces and cupboards. Pay special attention to room sizes, and beware of any that are given in square feet – that means the room is an odd shape. At the bottom of the list there will be the price, the rateable value and whether the property is freehold or leasehold.

Freehold or leasehold

When you buy freehold property you own the house and the ground it is built on. With leasehold property you pay ground rent to a landlord until the lease runs out. Most leases run for ninety-nine years, and under the Leasehold Reform Act 1967 you can sometimes buy the freehold at the end of the lease, or have it extended for fifty years.

Estate agents' literature

The language used in estate agents' literature is a mixture of semi-technical terms, a few old-fashioned ideas and downright sales jargon. Here is a short glossary of some of the language you will come up against:
Attractively priced ... it was over-priced in the first place and the seller has had to come down
Conveniently situated ... for what?
Ideal for development ... it is falling down
In a select area ... the rateable value is phenomenal
Interesting property ... interesting, that is, if you are looking for somewhere to keep chickens
Well situated for local transport ... it is on a busy main road.
   Some of the terms used to describe the property itself are often quaint, to say the least:
Elevations ... outside walls
Lobby ... the passageway leading from the front door
Pantry ... a cupboard in the kitchen (technically, a pantry is a cupboard you can walk into, not just a reasonably-sized cupboard)
Period-style ... mock-Tudor or -Georgian
Reception room ... living room
Residence ... (usually '*desirable*') it is huge

Bijou residence ... it is tiny
Outbuildings ... coal shed.
The garden may be described as being 'laid to lawn'; if it is not mentioned at all it is a wilderness.

Somewhere among all this heady stuff you may actually find something that interests you, but be prepared for many disappointments and disillusionments once you hit the house-hunting trail.

Once you have left your name and address with several estate agents, their literature will fall through your letter-box like leaves in autumn for the next few weeks, and you will soon have enough that looks interesting to proceed with the next step – looking at property. But in the meantime you can also make a study of newspaper advertisements and the specialist magazines such as *Dalton's Weekly*, *House Buyer*, *House Finder* and *Homefinder*. These magazines are particularly useful if you are looking for something in another part of the country. You can also make a tour of the area looking out for 'For Sale' boards. Do not be put off by the sign 'under offer': there is always the chance that the offer will not come to fruition, and you will get the next chance.

Having selected possibilities from estate agents' leaflets, and perhaps advertisements, make up a short list and place the properties in order of preference, then contact the estate agent or vendor, as the case may be, for an appointment to view.

4 Buying a Home: Taking a Look

'*Don't worry about the damp. You get used to it after a while.*'

Weekends are the best time to go house-hunting. Then you can visit several places and allow yourself plenty of time to look around. Do not try to visit too many in a short space of time, even though you may have a long list of possibilities. It is better to start with your top four and leave the others for another time, assuming you do not strike lucky in your first crop of selections. You may lose one or two chances that way

– the house-hunting trail is often rather crowded – but better that than making a lightning tour of a dozen or so houses with time only for a brief look at each. You are about to make a very large investment, so take your time about it.

If you can, take a friend or relative who has some knowledge or experience of house-hunting, such as a builder or surveyor or just someone who has done it all before. But do not turn up with an army of people ready to go swarming all over the house; it is, after all, private property and the owner will rightly resent being invaded. Should you decide to buy the property, you will be dealing with the vendor for some weeks to come and it is better to do so amicably. So do not start off by upsetting him, especially as a friendly relationship may pay off later when it comes to bargaining over the price or coming to an agreement regarding included items such as fitted carpets and semi-fixtures.

Assessing the property

When you arrive at the house, take a look at its immediate surroundings. How close are the neighbours? Is the house or garden overlooked by nearby premises? Is it well shielded from passers-by? Are there any potential sources of noise or smell close by, such as a factory or a farm?

Now study the house itself and see how closely it resembles the description of it that attracted you in the first place. You may be disappointed, but unless the description was blatantly dishonest do not be put off – the inside may be a lot better. If, after several minutes of contemplation, you get the feeling that this is not for you, do not sneak away without calling on the owner. Be fair, you have made an appointment so stick to it – just politely tell him you do not think it is what you are looking for and move on to the next place on your list.

If, however, you decide to go in, you will be given a tour of the house. As you go from room to room try to visualize how your furniture will look. It is a good idea to have a tape measure handy if you have any large items of furniture, so that you can be sure they will fit. Note also the layout of the house. Which rooms will get the most sun? Does the kitchen face north, the coolest side of the house, or does it get the full heat of mid-day? Take a notebook with you and jot down any points, good or bad, that you will want to remember. Otherwise, when you have visited all the houses on your list, you will find that you cannot recall which house had the new bathroom suite and which was the one with a damp patch in the front room.

If, after a good look round, your interest is aroused, ask to see heating bills covering a full year. If the house has an extension or outbuilding such as a garage, ask if planning permission was obtained (if it was not, you could be made to take it down). Ask to see invoices and guarantees for any building or repair work done recently. At this time you could also discuss any items that may be included such as carpets, light fittings and shelves. There may be some items the owner will be prepared to include in the price, but others he may be willing to sell as extras if you want them.

All fixtures, of course, are included in the price, but there is often confusion as to what is a fixture and what is a fitting. Generally speaking, all items permanently attached to any part of the house are fixtures, as are outbuildings with foundations, flower beds and trees. Light fittings such as shades and bulbs may be removed, but not the ceiling roses or flexes.

At the end of your visit, make an arrangement to call again for a more thorough inspection if what you have seen and heard has strengthened your interest. Make sure that the owner is aware that you will want to spend some time going over the house, and that you will need to go into the roof space and perhaps other out-of-the-way places, such as under the stairs and behind furniture which is against the walls. He should not object to this, and giving him advance warning of what you intend to do will help him minimize the inconvenience to himself and his family.

A thorough inspection of the house may well save you time and money, because if you leave it to the surveyor he might find faults that will put you off buying the place – and if they are faults that you could have spotted for yourself you will be faced with surveyor's fees that could have been avoided.

To carry out the inspection thoroughly and systematically you will need a checklist and a few tools. On your checklist, make up a separate page for the house exterior, each room, the hall, the stairs and the roof space. Under each heading list the points to be checked and have a remarks column down one side. The tools you will need are a screwdriver, penknife, steel tape measure, a torch or handlamp and a small mirror for looking into awkward corners. A pair of binoculars is also useful for checking the roof.

Roofing faults

Damp is the biggest single menace to property, so if possible carry out your inspection soon after a heavy rainfall when any weaknesses in the roof and outer walls will be revealed. First examine the roof for broken or dislodged tiles or slates. Pre-cast concrete and clay tiles have replaced slates during the past fifty years and are held in position by overlapping each other. They seldom move, but they sometimes crack or crumble due to frost action. Slates are held in position by nails, which in time rot away and allow the slates to slip or fall. If this 'nail sickness' is excessive the roof will need reslating, and more than likely some upstairs ceilings will be showing damp patches. Where only a few slates need replacing, asbestos-cement imitations are a reliable substitute for natural slates, which are expensive and difficult to obtain.

While checking the roof, look along the ridge – the apex of the roof – to see that it is not sagging and that the ridge tiles are not loose. Also have a look around the chimneystack: the space between the tiles and the chimney is sealed by a lead, zinc or bituminous felt strip, and if this is not tight against the chimney it will let water through. Any gaps can easily be sealed with a bitumastic sealant. If water has got through it will show as a damp patch on the chimney breast inside the house. The chimney should be capped if fireplaces have been bricked in, and the stack should be ventilated either by an air brick or by a curved capping tile.

There should also be an airbrick in a bricked up fireplace. Inadequate ventilation of the chimney will also cause damp patches on the chimney-breast due to condensation inside the flue.

The next areas to check are the guttering and downpipes. Plastic guttering is used in modern houses, and as replacement for cast-iron gutters on older property. It is generally troublefree but may develop leaks at the seals. These can be seen as accumulations of dirt on the underside of the gutter and close to the join. There should be a downpipe to every 20 feet of guttering for adequate drainage of rainwater, and the gutter should slope towards the downpipe by at least half an inch in every 10-foot run.

Drainage systems

There are two systems of domestic water drainage, the two-stack and the single stack. Since 1950 houses have been built with the single-stack system, where both lavatory and waste water outlets feed into a large-diameter vertical pipe outside the house. The earlier system had one pipe for waste water and another for lavatory drainage. In the two-stack system the lavatory, or 'soil', pipe is the larger of the two. The waste water pipe has a hopper head at its open top into which the bath and bathroom basin outlets are fed; at the bottom the pipe feeds into the same open gully as the kitchen sink outlet.

These stack pipes are usually made of cast-iron, which corrodes if it is not well-protected with paint. Because the pipes are set close to the wall, a poor painting job may have missed the back of the pipes, and eventually pinhole leaks occur and water will run directly on to the walls. Use the mirror to look behind the pipes, and if there are any areas of corrosion prod them with the penknife blade to see if the metal is thin.

Rising damp

After checking the roof and outside drainage system, turn your attention to the walls. Most pre-war houses have solid walls nine inches thick, and if the brickwork and mortar is in good condition this is adequate protection against rain. As an added protection, however, many houses are rendered with a coating of sand and cement finished with stone chippings. Look for cracks and bare patches, as these will allow water to creep in and spread behind the rendering, weakening it further and soaking into the brickwork. If the walls are not rendered check the brickwork for crumbling mortar joints. Both damaged rendering and faulty mortar joints can be repaired easily by a good builder, but if damp has penetrated through the walls they may need replastering on the inside.

Cavity walls in modern houses consist of two walls divided by a two-inch gap. The two walls are linked by metal ties placed at intervals, but if these have been bridged by loose mortar and brick chippings dropped by a careless bricklayer, moisture will penetrate to the inner wall and cause damp patches. Small areas of damp caused in this way can be cured by spraying the outside wall with a water-repellant liquid. Otherwise the only remedy is to knock holes in the wall and clear the ties by hand.

The most common type of damp, especially in old houses, is rising damp. It occurs because brickwork is porous and draws up moisture from the ground like a sponge, and to prevent this all houses built since 1875 have a damp-proof course (DPC) fitted. This can be recognized as a thick, black joint in the mortar about six inches from ground level. In old houses the DPC was made of slate, which being brittle tended to crack due to settlement. Modern damp-proof courses are made of flexible bituminous felt, which is built into both skins of a cavity wall. But this, too, can be bridged by mortar droppings inside the cavity.

Rising damp often occurs even when the DPC is perfectly sound, through the DPC being bridged by earth piled against the outside wall, or by a concrete path against the wall being built up too high. Follow the line of the DPC all round the house and see that nothing obscures it that could transfer moisture.

Below the level of the DPC there should be air-bricks set into the brickwork at intervals. This is to ventilate the underfloor space and prevent dry rot occurring. Check to see that they are all clear and unobstructed – some people block them off to prevent underfloor draughts – and get down on your knees and sniff round the aperture. A dank, musty smell will indicate dry rot in the floor joists or floorboards.

Dry rot and wet rot

Dry rot is an insidious, debilitating virus which will spread like a canker in house timbers if not treated quickly, and the only treatment is to replace all affected woodwork. The virus consists of spores which spread out tentacle-like strands that can penetrate brickwork in search of the moisture on which it thrives. Its effect is easy enough to spot, as the affected timber breaks up into rectangular-shaped pieces which will crumble to dust when you probe them with a penknife. Check all outside woodwork – window-frames, doors and if possible guttering fascia boards and roof gable-ends – and if you find dry rot, look for the fungus within a radius of at least 3 feet. It is recognizable as a grey-white growth with yellow patches and sometimes a rust-red centre.

The seriousness of dry rot cannot be over-emphasized. If you find it, point it out to the owner, who may not be aware of its existence, and ask if he is prepared to have it treated before selling the house. The building society's surveyor will almost certainly find it anyway, and may recommend that a loan should not be made unless the dry rot is eradicated.

Wet rot also thrives on damp, and is more common than dry rot, but less serious. Its fungus has thin, stringy strands of yellowish-brown which often appear as a veined pattern on the wood surface. When you probe wet rot-affected timber the knife will go in easily and the wood will break down into soggy fibres. Wet rot does not spread, and small areas can be cut out and treated with a fungicidal fluid, but badly rotted timbers must be replaced.

Settlement

Have a look for cracks in the walls running from the corners of windows and doorways. These are caused by settlement of the building over the years and are not serious if movement has ceased. Old cracks will have a weathered appearance, and you may see some that have been filled with mortar; but if the extreme ends of the cracks are fresh-looking then settlement is still taking place. If the house is more than five years old the cause should be sought, as normal settlement should have ceased.

Trees are a common cause of settlement. If there are large trees within 40 feet of the house, the moisture extracted by the roots causes the subsoil to shrink and the foundations will subside. Continuing settlement is difficult and expensive to cure, involving underpinning of the foundations, and a badly subsiding house is best left alone.

Damp and condensation

When you are satisfied that the house is structurally sound, on the outside at least, start your room-by-room inspection. Here again the first thing to look for is damp. Rising damp will show as stains on the wall spreading upwards from the skirting boards, and these should also be probed for wet rot and dry rot. If possible, lift the floor covering and examine the floorboards. In upstairs rooms look for stains on the ceiling, which will indicate a leaking roof. In the roof space examine any areas suspected of being damp in the light of what you have seen when checking the roof, and look for leaks around water pipes and the storage cistern. If the cistern is made of galvanized iron, check it for corrosion.

Another type of damp to watch out for, particularly in kitchens and bathrooms, is condensation. It occurs when moisture-laden air, such as steam, contacts a cold surface. It is most obvious on windows, but will also form on cold walls and appear as a black mould.

Condensation can be cured by adequate ventilation through an extractor fan fitted into the wall or window.

Woodworm

While inspecting timbers inside the house, keep a sharp lookout for woodworm, especially in floorboards and in the roof space. This is another deadly menace that must be dealt with quickly. The woodworm is, in fact, the grub of a flying beetle that lays its eggs on timber. The grub bores into the woodwork, where it stays for up to three years before turning into an adult beetle. Then it bites its way out of the wood, leaving a small, round hole. Clean holes, sometimes surrounded by finely powdered wood, show that the grubs are active, and although there may be only a few holes visible the timber could be riddled below the surface.

Like dry rot, woodworm requires specialist treatment, and if you find it you should ask the owner if he will either drop the price of the house or pay to have the treatment carried out.

Wiring circuits

By now you will have a pretty good idea whether the house is in good order or not. But before you go any further you should satisfy yourself that the electrical supply and the plumbing are in good condition.

Mains wiring in houses built pre-war was to the radial circuit system, which consists of separate cables for each power point radiating from the fuse box. It can be identified in two ways: by the number of fuses in the box – probably six or more – and by the power-point sockets, which have round-pin holes. Any house still wired to the radial system is long overdue for rewiring.

The modern method is the ring-main circuit, where a loop of cable serves all the power sockets. There are usually two loops, or rings, one for each floor of the house.

Lighting circuits also have two systems: the junction-box layout, used until the mid-1960s, and the loop-in system.

You can easily see which system has been used when you are in the roof space: in the loop-in system the cables run directly to the ceiling roses; in the junction-box system the cables run via junction boxes attached to the ceiling joists. The latter method is now outdated and this type of wiring would probably be due for renewal.

In all wiring layouts, look for the type of cable used. Modern cables are sheathed in grey PVC; formerly black rubber sheathing was used, but this perishes and deteriorates with age. In normal domestic conditions the life of rubber-sheathed wiring is about twenty years. Complete rewiring of a house can be very expensive, especially if it involves modernizing the system. Ask the owner if the wiring has been checked or rewired, or if any additions have been made, and if so when and by whom. For a guarantee that the work was carried out competently the contractor should have been approved by the National Inspection Council for Electrical Contracting (NICEC).

Plumbing systems

Next to electrical wiring, the plumbing system will probably be the most difficult aspect of the house for the layman to check. Basically, household plumbing serves two purposes: to bring water into the house and to take it out again as waste. The supply enters at the rising main, usually somewhere near the kitchen sink, and supplies fresh water to the kitchen tap, and then goes up to the cold-water storage cistern in the roof space. This cistern feeds all the other cold taps, the lavatory cistern and the hot-water cylinder. Hot water is taken from a pipe leading from the top of the cylinder, which may be heated by a boiler or by an immersion heater.

The water in a central heating system is entirely separate from that supplied to the taps. The same water circulates continuously and is topped up when necessary from the small feed and expansion tank in the roof space.

One of your main concerns will be the efficiency of the hot-water system. It is a good idea to ask the vendor to have the hot water and central heating systems running when you make your visit, even if you go on a hot summer's day. A poor supply of hot water may indicate scale in the boiler or cylinder, especially if heating is by an immersion heater: the elements become coated with scale and their efficiency is drastically reduced.

Check the central heating by running a hand over the radiators. If they are hot at the bottom but cold at the top then air locks are present, but these can be removed simply by bleeding the radiator. Cold patches, however, indicate blockages in the radiator which will require draining and flushing of the system. Ask the owner if the central heating system is regularly maintained (maintenance schemes are available for most systems) and when it was last overhauled.

In many pre-war houses the plumbing was installed after the house was built, with scant regard for our winter climate. Watch out for pipes on outer walls or running on the house's exterior. All such pipes should be well lagged as also should pipes in the roof space. The upstairs ceiling may be insulated, but the plumbing will be above the insulation and therefore not protected by it.

Copper has superseded lead in household plumbing since the war, so the presence of copper piping in a pre-war house shows that the system has been renewed or that additions have been made, particularly for 'plumbed-in' appliances such as dishwashers and washing machines. It is possible to join copper piping to lead piping, but most qualified plumbers advise complete replacement of lead by copper when making repairs or extensions to the system. If you see a mixture of copper and lead plumbing, suspect that the job was done 'on the cheap' and is liable to give trouble.

Making an offer

When you have completed your inspection, let the vendor know if you are likely to make an offer or not, but do not commit yourself until you have had time to think about it. Go away and study your checklist, weighing up the advantages and disadvantages of what you have seen. If you are keen to buy the place but have some doubts about its condition, make a note to ask your surveyor to pay special attention to any points worrying you. If there are major faults that need attention you can ask the vendor to reduce the price, though before settling on a final figure you should first find out how much the work will cost. It should be possible to obtain free estimates from most builders, electricians and plumbers and from roofing, damp-proofing and woodwork treatment specialists. Alternatively, you can ask the vendor to have the work done, in which case you would be prepared to meet his asking price, or something near it.

If you decide to go ahead with the purchase, contact either the vendor or the estate agent, by telephone or letter, and make an offer. Naturally you will want to get below the asking price if possible, so even if there is no question of any major repair work being necessary start by offering 5 per cent less. Do not be hustled by the owner's claim that six other people are also interested, but on the other hand do not risk losing the place by being too dogmatic. When you have agreed a price, confirm your offer in writing, but in all correspondence with the vendor include the words 'subject to contract'. This will allow you to withdraw your offer at any time up to exchange of contracts (see Chapter Six). The owner's or estate agent's confirmation of acceptance must be in writing and should come through a few days after the offer is made, provided of course that the offer *is* accepted.

Houses with vacant possession

It may be that the house you are hoping to buy has vacant possession, i.e. there is no one living there while it is up for sale. In such a case you will probably be dealing entirely through an estate agent. He will have keys for the house in his office and will either take you to see the place himself or, as in most cases, allow you to take the keys after signing for them. The advantage with vacant possession is that you can have a thorough look around without the embarrassment of the owner breathing down your neck, and there will be no furniture to move and probably no carpets to lift. You may well be able to carry out a full inspection on your first visit so that you do not need to return. One disadvantage is that you will not be able to ask about fuel bills, etc. The estate agent may be able to tell you a little about the house, but not about its running costs, and the mains services will probably be disconnected so you will not be able to check central heating, hot-water supply and electrical supplies.

This was a snag that Andrew and Auriol encountered, and one that worked out to their considerable disadvantage. The house they bought had a large, gas-fired water heater which supplied the kitchen, bathroom and the washbasin in the upstairs toilet. But when they looked at the house the gas supply had been disconnected, so they were unable to test the heater. Since the house had been re-possessed by the building society it was not possible to get in touch with the previous owner, and the estate agent was unable to give an assurance that the heater worked. But it looked okay, so the couple took a chance – and lost. The heater did not work, and would have cost as much to repair as the price of a new one. Furthermore, it would have had to be resited: it was on an inner wall, and since it had been installed new regulations had come into force requiring gas heaters to be on an outer wall.

Having used up most of their savings in buying the house, Andrew and Auriol were forced to spend several weeks, in the middle of winter, without hot water. And when they had managed to save enough for a new water heater, costing £120, they found they had to pay an installation charge amounting to £113 on top.

The lesson to be learned from this is clear: if you are

thinking of buying a house with vacant possession and cannot try out any equipment that could be expensive to replace, consider very carefully whether to proceed any further. This is where the head has to rule the heart, because the house may be just what you are looking for in all other respects. You could try getting a reduction in the price, or ask the estate agent if he could arrange to have the equipment tested, otherwise you must make up your mind whether to take a chance or move on in your search.

Bargaining

Chris and Catherine also bought a house with vacant possession – a house they had fallen in love with until Chris went into the loft and saw daylight through the roof. Close examination showed that several tiles were missing and others had moved. A builder friend assured them that it was not a serious problem, and they decided to make an offer but use the faulty roof as a bargaining point. Chris suggested offering £500 below the asking price, and Catherine argued that the offer should be made *with the condition that the roof be repaired at the owner's expense.* The estate agent agreed that this was a fair offer, and persuaded the owner to accept it.

There may be a number of reasons why a house is for sale with vacant possession, and it is worth finding out from the estate agent. It may be that the owner has moved to another house and has taken out a bridging loan, in which case he will be paying high interest rates and will be keen to make a quick sale. Or he may have been left the property in a will and be anxious to turn his inheritance into cash. These are conditions that will work in your favour when you come to bargain over the price.

Conservation areas

One final word of warning: if the house you intend to buy is in a conservation area you may be restricted in any repairs or improvements you wish to carry out. You will not, for example, be allowed to cut down any trees (the penalty for doing so is a fine based on twice the estimated value of the tree). Nor may you demolish any building without permission, even if it is about to fall down (the fine for illegal demolition of a building is £400). If you want to make any alterations or extensions to the house you must ask the local authority for permission, and that applies even to changing the roofing tiles. Slate tiles used on older buildings are becoming increasingly difficult and expensive to obtain, but you may find that the local authority will insist that the house be retiled as it was originally.

The owner of the house should know if a conservation order has been made, or you can find out from the local council planning office.

5 Buying a Recently-built House

'You see, I did notify him in writing.'

When you buy a brand-new house, or one that is less than ten years old, you will receive a House Purchaser's Agreement issued by the National House-Building Council (NHBC). This agreement covers all major defects arising during the first ten years of the property's life and is usually known as the 'ten-year guarantee'. The agreement is made between the buyer and the vendor, who may be a builder or developer.

During the first two years the vendor agrees to put right any major defects, and from the third to tenth year the NHBC takes over the responsibility. But how good is the guarantee? What does it cover? How do you make a claim? And how does the NHBC operate?

The National House-Building Council

The NHBC is a government-approved body, and its council members are nominated from various groups associated with the building and selling of houses. It includes employers, trade union representatives, architects, surveyors, estate agents, local government officers, consumer groups, town planners and health officers. The Ministry of Housing and Construction and the Greater London Council appoint observers, and the chairman is appointed by the Secretary of State for the Environment.

The NHBC has a register of builders and developers whose work, and financial standing, has been subjected to stringent examinations.

When a builder applies to join the register he must submit houses currently under construction by him for a technical inspection by the Council. His work is then graded as good, satisfactory or poor. For evidence of financial stability, the council requires a banker's reference or a payment of £200 for each dwelling, which is returned with interest if the builder is accepted for the register.

Once on the register, the builder is given a copy of the NHBC Handbook which, in Part I, defines the rules, the Code of Practice and the Code of Conduct; Part II is the technical guide, which lays down the standards to which houses are to be built. Failure to meet these standards, legal or technical, can lead to the builder's expulsion from the register, and because most building societies will grant mortgages only on new houses carrying the NHBC guarantee, expulsion sounds the death-knell for a builder. The incentive to maintain a high standard is therefore strong, and there are other safeguards which keep builders on their toes – in some cases the NHBC issues a warning if a builder's standards start to fall, and sometimes a higher inspection fee is charged as a forceful hint that an improvement is required.

To keep up their high standards the NHBC has site inspectors based at regional offices in England, Scotland, Wales and Northern Ireland. The inspectors are men who have spent at least three years working on building sites and know every trick of the trade, every bodge and dodge in the business. They visit houses under construction at the foundations stage, and then regularly and frequently during the early stages when the most serious defects are likely to occur (such as misplaced damp-proof courses, dirty wall cavities and undersized roof and floor timbers).

If the inspector finds a fault he points it out to the site foreman, and it must be rectified to the inspector's satisfaction before he will grant a certificate for the house. Without that certificate the builder cannot draw up a House Purchaser's Agreement.

Even with these stringent tests, there are still some builders who are better, or worse, than others. Some will provide a service and standard higher than required by the NHBC, others will meet the bare requirements necessary to obtain the Certificate. The NHBC will not recommend individual building firms, so it is up to the buyer to find out as much as he can about the builder's reputation. This is best done by talking to people on a recently built estate; most people love to show off their new home, even to strangers, and will be quick to point out any faults. If you visit an estate of new houses and spot one that is already up for sale again, knock and ask why.

If the estate is so new that no houses are complete and occupied, have a good look around the site. There are many signs of a good or bad builder that even the inexperienced eye can spot. Watch out for the way materials are stored - window frames and timbers should be stacked off the ground and covered with tarpaulins. Look for tidiness - a site littered with empty paint cans, discarded packing material and empty cement bags points to untidy workmen and poor supervision, both hallmarks of the bad builder.

You may wonder why, if the NHBC inspection is so thorough, the prospective buyer should have to do his own investigating. The answer is simply because the NHBC system is not foolproof, nor does it claim to be. The Council expels an average of forty builders each year, but it takes time to spot a bad builder and take action against him, and in the meantime he will be continuing to build and sell houses. Of course, anyone unfortunate enough to buy from a bad builder has the ten-year guarantee for protection, but that will not compensate for the frustrations and inconveniences suffered before things are put right.

To be absolutely certain you can, if you wish, engage your own surveyor to keep an eye on things when you are having a house built. This can be a wise move if you are asking for any special features requiring standards not governed by the NHBC: for example, if you are having expensive equipment built into a fully-fitted kitchen.

A private survey will not in any way affect the issuing of an NHBC guarantee.

The House Purchaser's Agreement

The House Purchaser's Agreement defines what is covered by the guarantee and what is excluded, but, as for most legal documents, some clarification is helpful. Indeed, it is important to know just what is covered and what is not, as the NHBC charges an investigation fee of £40. The fee is returned if the claim is valid, or it may be returned if the NHBC considers the claim to have been reasonable though not within the terms of the guarantee. The fee is not returned, however, if the claim is not justified. The NHBC's decision on this is final: it will not enter into correspondence.

Basically the defects for which a builder is responsible are faults arising from non-compliance with the NHBC's minimum standards. These could be subsidence due to poor foundations, dry rot in timbers, structural weaknesses in the roof or walls, and poor finishing.

How to make a claim

Defects must be reported to the builder *in writing* if they appear during the first two years, and as soon as possible after they are discovered. The Council stresses the importance of reporting defects at once and in writing. The explanatory notes in the Agreement state quite clearly: 'You must report defects as soon as practical after they appear. You cannot complain about finishing defects for the first time months after you have entered the house.' A further note points out that 'A valid claim may fail at a later date if you cannot prove that you notified the vendor in writing within the initial guarantee period.'

That would seem to be clear enough, but many people merely point out defects to a site foreman and then complain to the NHBC when nothing is done. This enables the builder to claim that he was not aware of any faults, since he had not been notified in writing, and to get out of his responsibility.

If, after being notified of a defect in writing, the builder does not carry out repairs, the purchaser should then write to the NHBC's Conciliation Office, which will then instruct the builder to take prompt action. If this fails to produce results the purchaser will be asked to make a formal application for inspection, enclosing a £40 deposit, and if the NHBC inspector considers the claim valid the builder will be given thirty to sixty days to put the defect right. Nearly 3,000 complaints are investigated by the NHBC each year, and in most cases the ruling is given in favour of the purchaser.

One common complaint which is not upheld concerns shrinkage. All houses 'shrink' as bricks, mortar and plaster dry out, and the builder cannot be blamed for it. During the first year after completion, cracks will appear in plasterwork which may seem alarming but are quite normal. If, however, cracks continue to appear after the first year then a complaint might be justified.

The NHBC's liability, from the third to tenth years, is limited to major damage due to defects in the load-bearing structure. The emphasis is on *major damage*, which the NHBC defines as 'unusual calamities such as major settlement or subsidence, dry rot causing structural failure, or chemical failure of structural elements.' The guarantee does not cover the kinds of defects which appear in houses in the course of time, such as loose or cracked roofing tiles. And it does not cover rising damp through a faulty damp-proof course if it appears after two years and is not itself causing a major structural defect.

The value of the guarantee

It seems, then, that the house would have to be literally falling apart for the NHBC to accept a claim. So of what use is the guarantee? And why does the NHBC not accept responsibility for all defects?

The short answer to the first question is that any guarantee is better than no guarantee at all, and though the liability may be limited, it does at least cover the sort of defects that could otherwise involve the householder in enormous costs. The reason why the NHBC cannot take full responsibility for all defects is simply that they do not build houses: only a builder can be made responsible for his product, and after two years he is clear of all liability. And although the NHBC's inspections may be thorough, some faults can and do go undetected occasionally. That is why it is important to keep a good look-out for structural faults during the first two years, and have them put right by the builder.

There is another aspect of the ten-year guarantee, however, which is perhaps more important than the cover for structural faults. It covers the purchaser against the bankruptcy of the builder.

Although the NHBC takes care to see that members on its register are financially sound, it cannot foresee building slumps, bank crises and economic cutbacks. In 1974, when a lending freeze and the collapse of several small banks caused more than 1,000 builders to go out of business, the NHBC was able to help many home-buyers whose builders had gone bankrupt.

In cases of bankruptcy the NHBC guarantees to pay for major defects that a builder, because of his bankruptcy, is unable to remedy. It will also look at any house that has minor defects if their cumulative effect reduces the value of the house to below what was paid for it.

As mentioned earlier, you will receive a House Purchaser's Agreement when you buy a house less than ten years old. It should be passed over to you with all other documents concerning the house by the owner or his solicitor. You are then covered for the period which the guarantee has still to run, with exactly the same cover as if you had bought the house new: for example, if the house is only one year old the builder is still responsible for faults occurring during the following year. But when buying second-hand you *must* have the property surveyed by your own surveyor. The NHBC will not pay for major defects that were visible when you bought the house.

6 Buying a Home: Wheels in Motion

'If we'd used a solicitor we would have found out about the public footpath.'

The transfer of property from one person to another is called conveyancing, and so complex is the transaction that it is usually necessary to engage a solicitor to make the wheels turn smoothly. Solicitors, like doctors, are not allowed to advertise their services, so you will not find them listed in the Yellow Pages or in the ads column of your local newspaper. How, then, should you set about finding a solicitor who will act for you reliably, speedily and at a reasonable cost?

You may be able to find a good solicitor by personal recommendation, from a friend or relative who has recently bought or sold a house. Failing that your building society manager, bank manager or estate agent will be able to put you on to a reliable firm. You can obtain a list of local solicitors from the Citizens' Advice Bureau, but they will not recommend any particular firm.

There are no fixed fees for conveyancing, so it pays to shop around. What you will have to pay a solicitor depends on the value of the property you are buying - the higher the value the more he will charge - and the complexity of the transaction. So when you ask a solicitor for an estimate of his costs, make sure he knows exactly what he will be dealing with so that he can give a fair assessment. Before you finally decide on your solicitor, however, ask if he is on the panel of solicitors held by your building society. If he is, it will save you money because building societies engage a solicitor to investigate the property they are lending money on, and if your solicitor acts for both you and the society you pay only one fee for that service. If, on the other hand, the building society engages a solicitor other than yours you have to pay his fee as well.

What a conveyancing solicitor does

The role of your solicitor is to advise you and act on your behalf, but, at all time he acts on your instructions which must, therefore, be clear and precise. From the start, make sure he has all the information he needs: if he has to write to you or phone you for information you have failed to give him, it will all go down on your bill. Similarly, do not keep ringing him to find how things are going - every time he picks up the phone it will cost you money.

On your first visit he will want to know all the details about the house you intend to buy, and a few about yourself, namely:
(1) your full name, address and occupation

(2) the address of the house, the owner's name and the name of his solicitor
(3) the price of the house and whether it is freehold or leasehold
(4) the name and address of the estate agent, if any
(5) details of your mortgage (it is best to have arranged this before going to the solicitor)
(6) what fixtures or extras are included in the sale
(7) the date you would like to move in.

In addition to those basic details there could be other useful information you can supply. For example, you may have been able to find out from a neighbour whether there have been any disputes arising from rights of way, ill-defined boundaries or responsibility for fences. If there have been disputes, your solicitor will ask the vendor's solicitor for details, which he must supply. He is not, however, obliged to volunteer such information, and probably will not do so if it is likely to prejudice his client's chances of selling the house.

At an early stage in the transaction the vendor may ask for a preliminary deposit, sometimes called 'an advance on the deposit'. (This should not be confused with the deposit of 5-20 per cent which is the balance between the amount loaned to you and the full price of the house, paid through your solicitor when contracts are exchanged.) A preliminary deposit has no legal standing, and you are not obliged to pay it. Even if you do, it is no guarantee that the house will be yours, because the vendor can return the deposit if he wishes to withdraw from the transaction for any reason.

If the vendor insists on a deposit, however, make a small payment of, say, £25, but do not pay it to him direct. You can pay it through the estate agent, and you should ask for a receipt specifying that the agent is 'stakeholder for the vendor', not 'agent for the vendor'. As stakeholder, the agent cannot hand over the money to the vendor, and he must return it to you if the sale is not completed.

Most sales are completed four weeks after contracts have been exchanged, but a lot of water flows under the bridge before then and there are many things that can go wrong. One common delay occurs when the vendor finds that the house *he* is hoping to buy is no longer available for some reason or other, so he holds up the sale of his house, or may withdraw from the transaction altogether. The buying and selling of property often involves a long chain of buyers and sellers, and it needs only one person along the line to withdraw - perhaps because he or she fails to obtain a mortgage - for the whole sequence to collapse. If all goes well, however, you should be able to move into your home within two to three months of starting the transaction, but do not make any definite moves, such as buying carpets and curtains, until contracts have been exchanged.

The contract

Two copies of the contract are drawn up, by the vendor's solicitor. He sends one copy to your solicitor who, when he has checked the contract and is satisfied that all is in order, will arrange for you and the vendor to sign the two copies simultaneously and exchange them. At this stage both you and the vendor become legally committed to go ahead with the transaction.

Checking the contractual details, particularly the rights to the property, is a major part of your solicitor's service, part of which is commonly referred to as 'carrying out a search'. He will send a list of questions to the vendor's solicitor seeking to confirm, amongst other things, the vendor's right to sell, and that he is not leaving a mortgage outstanding. He will also ensure that there is no 'statutory tenant' in the house who cannot be evicted. Your solicitor will find out if there are any rights over the property, such as the right of a neighbour to cross the land or share a drive. He will inform you of any such rights, and it will be up to you to decide whether they are acceptable or not. Similarly the solicitor will find what rights you may or may not have over surrounding property. For example, when Chris and Catherine went to view their house they saw at the rear of the terraced row a block of lock-up garages with a large forecourt extending to the rear of the gardens. The entrance to the forecourt had a lockable post to prevent unauthorized parking, and all owners of the houses in the row had a key. It seemed safe to assume, therefore, that the keyholders could park their cars on the forecourt, but this was not so: access to the forecourt was only a right of way to the gardens' back entrances.

There may also be covenants, which are restrictions on the use of the land or the house usually dating back many years. There may well be a covenant against anyone using the house for carrying on any kind of business, so plans for providing 'bed and breakfast', for example, could be thwarted even if the local planning authority approves. On new housing estates, restrictions are often imposed on the keeping of poultry and on the keeping of boats or caravans on the property.

The vendor's solicitor must give truthful and accurate answers to your solicitor's questions. If any information he gives is later found to be incorrect, you can sue the vendor for damages.

Another task your solicitor will perform is to send a list of questions to the local authority asking whether there are any major development schemes in the offing, such as compulsory purchase for a road or motorway project, or a development of the area that might include industrial buildings. He will also check that planning permission was obtained for any extensions to the house – or outbuildings – which are subject to planning laws. Planning permission from the local council is required for some new buildings and additions to buildings, and must have been obtained *before* the work was commenced. If the house you buy has had any such work done without permission, you could be made to take it down.

You may be hoping to make additions to the house yourself, or put up a garage, and if so you should tell your solicitor of your intentions. He will then find out whether planning permission will be needed and whether it is likely to be given.

Not until he is satisfied that the vendor's contract is in order, and that there are no restrictive covenants or likely developments that could cause you trouble later, will your solicitor ask you to sign the contract.

Solicitors' fees

The solicitor's costs break down into two parts: the payments he makes on your behalf and his own charges for work done by him. The payments he makes will include a fee to the local council for the search, and also a fee to the Land Registry. In many parts of the country, land registration is compulsory, which means that unregistered land must be registered when the house changes hands. The fee depends on the purchase price. If the property you are buying is already registered, your solicitor will arrange for the registration to be transferred to your name, for which there is also a (lower) fee.

Another payment he will make is Stamp Duty, payable to the Inland Revenue, which is never short of ideas for parting us from our money. The duty is a percentage of the purchase price, but there is a lower limit below which duty is not paid; after that it rises in steps of half a percent. Stamp Duty charges change from time to time, so you should ask your solicitor what the current charges are. You will be able to save a considerable amount of money if you can achieve a lower purchase price and thereby fit into a lower 'band' or rating by coming to an arrangement with the vendor over fittings. For example, if the house is priced at £30,500 inclusive of fittings and the Stamp Duty goes from half a per cent to one per cent above £30,000 you may be able to persuade the vendor to reduce the price to £30,000 plus a separate payment of £500 for the fittings, which are not subject to Stamp Duty.

If you have not already made arrangements for a mortgage before seeing your solicitor, he can arrange one for you - providing, of course, that you can meet all the requirements of a building society. But this will be an extra charge in his fees, and in any case you would be wise to make sure that a mortgage is available long before you reach the stage of engaging a solicitor. If you have done so, then finalizing the mortgage should be your next step. Make an early visit to your building society manager to complete the mortgage application form, and at this time you will probably be asked to pay the valuation survey fee. Building societies are required by the Building Societies Act to obtain a written valuation in respect of any property on which they extend a loan. And it must be stressed that the survey is purely a valuation: it is not a full structural survey so do not make the mistake of thinking that if the house passes its valuation survey there is no need for you to engage your own surveyor.

The Homeloan scheme

At this time you may also be able to take advantage of the government's Homeloan scheme. This scheme was introduced in 1978 to help first-time buyers and provides a tax-free bonus if you have been saving for two years. Your savings could be with a building society, National Savings Bank, a bank deposit account or National Savings Save-As-You-Earn. The amount of the bonus depends on how much you have saved, and there are a number of restrictions which may vary from time to time. But you may be entitled to a sum at least large enough to pay off one of your commitments, such as your surveyor's or solicitor's fees. You can obtain up-to-date details of the scheme from a building society, bank or post office.

Engaging a surveyor

You can choose your surveyor on the strength of personal recommendation or on the advice of your building society or estate agent. It is possible to use the same surveyor as the building society, and you may save a little on his fee if he carries out your survey at the same time as the valuation survey. As with engaging a solicitor, shop around and get estimates.

You should also instruct your surveyor, specifying that you want a full *structural* survey. You are not interested in the sizes of the rooms, whether the place has central heating or not and how many power points there are in the kitchen. You will have seen all that for yourself, but some surveyors tend to pad out their reports with unnecessary information. Tell him of any particular points you want him to give special attention to in the light of your own inspection. But if you have suspected rising damp or woodwork diseases (dry rot, wet rot and woodworm) you can arrange a free inspection from most of the large specialist firms: a list of names can be obtained from the British Wood Preserving Association and the British Chemical Dampcourses Association (see Appendix).

If you have arranged any such free inspections, tell the surveyor so that he will not duplicate the inspection. In his survey he may also recommend a separate inspection of electrical wiring and drains. These you will have to pay extra for, but the Electricity Board in some areas will carry out a low-cost inspection for prospective customers. To take advantage of this, however, you will need to have completed the purchase of the house and applied to the Electricity Board for connection to the supply.

When you receive your surveyor's report, make sure he has done everything you asked; if he has not, withhold his fee until he has completed the job to your satisfaction.

Of course, if you are buying brand-new property you will not need a surveyor because the house will almost certainly be covered by the ten-year guarantee of the National House-Building Council (see Chapter Five). If the house is not new but has been built within the last ten years, i.e. it is still covered by the guarantee, it is still worthwhile having it surveyed, because the guarantee does not cover faults which are not considered major defects, or have not arisen from bad workmanship: for example, faults caused by neglect or misuse on the part of the owner.

Is your surveyor really necessary?

Generally speaking, the older a house the more important it is to have it surveyed. But there are sometimes circumstances in which a surveyor's services, and his fee, are dispensable. For example, if you are buying a house from someone who has occupied it for only a few years, ask if it was surveyed when he bought it and ask to see the surveyor's report. Remember that what you are mostly concerned with is any structural fault that could be very expensive to put right, and if any such fault existed when the house was last surveyed you can find out easily enough if it has been rectified – either by asking the owner, who should produce bills as evidence, or looking for yourself. But if the house was given a clean bill of health within the last five years it is hardly likely that any major faults will have developed during that time.

To survey or not to survey is a vexed question, and surveyors themselves have tended to make people wonder if they are necessary by making lengthy, padded-out and often incomplete reports. Extracts from recent survey reports have included the following statements: 'the house is constructed of brick and the roof is tiled'; 'electricity is supplied by the Electricity Board'; 'the house is one mile from the railway station'. Frequently a report will say that floor-boards could not be inspected because of fitted carpets, or the roof space was in good order 'as far as could be seen' – in other words, the surveyor only poked his head through the hatchway.

Quite often the more padded a report is, the better the house, because the surveyor is trying to justify his high fee. A surveyor's report can be useful, however, in lowering the price of the house if, for example, the roof needs retiling. Try to get an estimate for this from a builder, and subtract that amount from the vendor's asking price, or ask the vendor to have the work done before you exchange contracts.

Avoiding a contracts race

It sometimes happens that more than one person negotiates a house purchase at the same time. Solicitors call this a contracts race, and it can be a very unsporting event. It usually happens because the vendor has placed his house in the hands of several estate agents, and then continues to accept offers through all of them. The first the prospective buyers hear of it is through their solicitors, who then refer to their clients for instructions as to whether to proceed or not. A solicitor will not usually advise you in such circumstances. You must make up your own mind whether to risk going ahead and possibly being beaten to the post. In a contracts race the vendor holds all the cards; only he and his solicitor know how far advanced each individual transaction has progressed, and they will try to push things along by implying that someone is about to exchange contracts. They may not actually suggest that you stand a better chance if you increase your offer, but it will be implied. Unless you are prepared to risk losing several hundreds of pounds in solicitors' and surveyors' fees, remove yourself from the contracts race as soon as possible. He who fights and runs away ...

If, however, you have set your heart on the house and are willing to take the risk, then do all you can to speed things along. Your solicitor will pull out all the stops, because winning the race on your behalf will be a matter of professional pride to him. You should also ask your building society manager to get the mortgage through as quickly as possible. Similarly, put your surveyor to work as soon as you can. If you are using the building society's surveyor, as suggested earlier, this will save time. But do not cut corners, and do not allow yourself to be panicked. Remember, too, that as a first-time buyer you may have a slight edge on your rivals, who may be involved in selling their own property as well as competing with you.

Completion

The final step in the transaction is completion, when your solicitor hands over your deposit and the building society pays the money it is lending. Your solicitor will have a final look at the title deeds, which will then be held by the building society until you have paid off the mortgage, and he will check the rates receipt, produced by the vendor's solicitor, to see that the rates have been paid up to date. When he is satisfied that all is well and that the vendor's solicitor has received the money for his client, the house is yours. A few days later you will receive your solicitor's bill, which should be close to the estimate he gave. If it is appreciably higher, ask him why, and if you are not satisfied with his answer ask him for a Remuneration Certificate from the Law Society. Do this *before* you pay the bill. Your solicitor must then submit the papers to the Law Society for inspection and they will decide whether you have been overcharged or not. If the Law Society rules in your favour, the solicitor must abide by that ruling and charge the amount fixed by them. You can ask for a Remuneration Certificate even if your bill does not exceed the estimate, if on reflection you consider it was too high in the first place.

Cut-price conveyancing

You can, of course, dispense with a solicitor's fees by doing the conveyancing yourself, though you will still have to pay the building society's solicitor's fees. For first-time buyers, however, do-it-yourself conveyancing can be extremely hazardous. While it is simple enough to carry out such requirements as the local authority and land registry searches, you will be up against professionals when dealing with an estate agent and the vendor's solicitor. Problems may arise that only an experienced house-buyer or a qualified solicitor would know how to cope with. You may end up going to a solicitor to get yourself out of a tangle, which could cost you more than if you had engaged a solicitor in the beginning.

Another way of cutting conveyancing costs is to go to a conveyancing organization: they can be much cheaper than a solicitor, and some claim that they can reduce your costs by at least half. The Law Society disapproves of conveyancing organizations – an understandable attitude since it is concerned with the livelihood of its members – and points out that solicitors are professionally qualified. And so they are, but professional qualifications are not needed for conveyancing if it is carried out by experienced people, and there is no reason why you should not at least approach one of the organizations to see what they offer. The National Association of Conveyancers (see Appendix) will supply a list of their members.

One word of warning about self-conveyancing: be wary of a house vendor who is doing his own and suggests you do the same 'to save legal costs'. It is often in the vendor's interest to deal with a purchaser who is doing his own conveyancing and lacks the skill to probe vague or ambiguous answers to his enquiries.

Conveyancing in Scotland

In Scotland they do things differently and, as so often with the Scots, apparently more sensibly. North of the Border, although estate agents do exist, most properties are bought through solicitors, who also act as estate agents and operate through a Solicitors' Property Centre. Here you will find details of property just as you would in an estate agent's office in England.

The chief difference between buying a home in Scotland and buying one in England is that in Scotland you do not make an offer 'subject to contract'. A written offer is made and is binding, providing it is also accepted in writing. Before making an offer, therefore, you must complete all the preliminary stages such as finalizing a mortgage and having the property surveyed. The local authority search is made by the vendor's solicitor.

Your written offer is known as a 'missive of sale', and may be one of many. This is where life can get a bit fraught, for although it is not quite the same as a contracts race in England you are more often than not in competition with other prospective buyers. The vendor usually sets a time-limit for offers, and instructs his solicitor to accept the highest bid made in that time. You are not allowed to know what other bids have been made, which prevents the sale from becoming an auction, so it is rather like playing a hand of poker in the dark.

There is no land registration in Scotland, but all property is recorded in the Sasine Register which is kept in Edinburgh. It is open to public inspection, but entries do not guarantee that the title is legally valid.

English home-buyers, and sellers, may envy the Scottish system – and at its best it works well. A Mr Andrew Walker of Galston in Ayrshire tells how he bought a house in one week: he and his wife viewed the house on a Saturday afternoon, had it surveyed the following Tuesday and made an offer the next day; by mid-day on Friday the offer had been accepted.

Mr Skyring, living in the Shetland Isles, tells a different story however. He points out that every time you bid for a house you have to engage a solicitor and surveyor before you make the bid, and you have no way of knowing if the bid will be successful. He quotes the case of one person who bid unsuccessfully for nine houses, resulting in tremendous costs all to no avail. At the tenth attempt he was lucky, but then found that he had paid £7000 more than the next highest bid.

7 Moving in

'Wouldn't it have been easier to have sent change-of-address cards?'

Congratulations! The days of waiting and wondering are over, and you are about to move into your first home. How you go about the move will play an important part in the smooth running of your home in the early days. If done in a hurry, without care and forethought, your delight in taking possession of your own home could turn to frustration and misery.

Preparing the house

Unless circumstances dictate otherwise, do not be in a hurry to move in. If you are a tenant you will, of course, want to get into your new home quickly because you have started paying rent on it. But even so, allow yourself a few days for the move so that you can get the place reasonably straight before you settle in. If you have bought the property you can take a little longer, and the first thing you will need to do is get busy with mop and pail. However tidy the previous owner may have been there is bound to be some cleaning to do. You may also want to do some redecorating, and with the house empty you will never again have a better chance to paint and paper without having to move furniture around and protect carpets.

Now, too, is the time to get carpets and lino laid. If any of your rooms are awkwardly shaped it will be worth your while to have the work done by professionals.

Hiring a van

As it is your first home, you will not have the problem of shifting a houseful of furniture from your old home to the new, but you will probably have acquired a few essential items such as bed-linen, cutlery, tableware and the like, and there will of course be your clothes to move. A small van will be useful, and if you do not have one or cannot borrow one from a friend, you can hire one from a rental firm. Like car rental, however, van hire can be expensive and you should plan to rent it for as short a time as possible. Have everything ready to load before you collect the vehicle and make as few trips as possible, returning the van immediately after the last journey. Try to make the move on a week-day or a Saturday morning as some hire firms close on a Saturday afternoon and few are open on a Sunday.

The bulk of your furniture, however, is likely to be newly bought and will be delivered by the furniture company, so you should decide exactly where everything is to go and get the delivery men to place each item in the appropriate rooms. Nowadays a great deal of contemporary furniture comes in packages and the buyer is expected to assemble it, but you could be lucky enough to find some soft-hearted delivery men to do the job for you. It is worth a try!

Connecting supplies

Gas appliances must be fitted by Gas Board fitters, or by fitters approved by the Gas Board. It is illegal for you, or anyone not so approved, to connect a gas appliance. Give your local gas showrooms at least two weeks' notice. If you are buying new appliances, they can be assembled and connected at the same time as delivery.

An electric cooker must have its own power point, with a separate fuse in the main fuse-box. Arrange to have this fitted by a qualified electrician if no such installation already exists. You may also need to have a washing machine or dishwasher plumbed in to the water supply and drainage system. These are jobs within the scope of a handyman, otherwise a qualified plumber should be engaged for the work.

Gas, electricity and water supplies will probably have been disconnected if the house has been empty for some time, and you should notify the relevant authorities at least one week before you want the supplies reconnected; in the case of gas and electricity, ask for the meters to be read at the same time. You should try to be present when the supplies are reconnected, because in each case the installations will be checked to see that they are in order, and they will not be connected if there are any faults which could be dangerous. These will be pointed out to you by the gas, water or electricity board's representative so that you can get them put right.

If the house has a telephone installed, ask the local sales office to reconnect it, or arrange with the previous owner to leave it connected and have the bill rendered on the day he moves out; by doing this you will save the reconnection charge.

You may have to wait some time if you want a new telephone installed; the sales office will tell you how long you may have to wait, and will advise you on the different types of installation available and what they cost. You do not need to fill in an application form for a new telephone; you can place your order by a phone call.

Redirecting mail

The Post Office will require seven days' notice for redirection of mail. Fill in form P944G, which you can get from any post office, and your post will be redirected for a period of one month, three months or a year, as required, on payment of a small charge. Forms are also available at post offices for notifying a change of address for your personal giro and Premium Bonds.

To make sure that mail starts coming to you direct as soon as possible, notify everyone who is likely to write to you well before you move in. You will be surprised how many people there are to inform: apart from relatives and friends there are the clubs, societies and organizations (AA or RAC, for example) of which you may be a member. In addition you will need to notify your employer, insurance companies, hire-purchase companies, your bank, any publications to which you subscribe (newspapers, trade journals, etc.) and book or record clubs.

All those mentioned can be notified by sending change-of-address cards, which you can buy at stationers, but there are special arrangements for notifying some government bodies. The DHSS will require not only your address but also your date of birth and your National Insurance number. To change the address on your motor vehicle licence, if you have the old type of logbook you must notify the local office where the vehicle was registered. For the new type of registration document you must apply in writing to the Vehicle Licensing Centre, Swansea, SA99 1AB. You must also send your driving licence to Swansea with your new address in Section 1 on the reverse side of the licence. A new licence will be issued free of charge, but failure to notify a change of address on a driving licence could render you liable to a fine of up to £20.

You must also write to the Department of Inland Revenue, the address of which is shown on your income tax notice of coding.

Finding a doctor and a dentist

If you are not moving to a new district you need only inform your doctor and dentist of the new address. Otherwise you must de-register with your doctor and find one in the area in which you will be living. The local Family Practitioners' Committee (whose address is available from the Citizens' Advice Bureau) will be able to give you the name of a doctor who can accept you in his practice. Take your medical card to your new doctor and he will arrange for your records to be transferred. To find a new dentist, look for the list displayed in the local post office or library. While in the library you may want to apply for a ticket, but do not forget to return books and cancel tickets at your old library.

Before moving in it is a good idea to stock up with a few groceries, etc., so that you will not have to worry about shopping during the first few days in your home. You will also need to contact local tradesmen for deliveries such as milk, bread and newspapers.

Finally, if you are going to travel a long distance by car, make sure the vehicle is fully serviced, and if you are planning to load it heavily, increase the tyre pressures in accordance with the car handbook. Check your route, and if you are intending to make an overnight stop on the way, book the accommodation well in advance.

8 Peace of Mind

'When it came to rebuilding it after the fire we found we were rather under-insured.'

Even before you move into your home you will need to take out some insurance. Whoever is lending you the money for the mortgage will insist that you insure the 'bricks and mortar': this is known as a buildings policy. Most building societies also require a mortgage guarantee policy for first-time buyers borrowing more than 80 per cent; the cost is usually 3-4 per cent of the amount in excess of 80 per cent and the premium is a once-only payment which can be added to your loan. A mortgage guarantee, or indemnity, policy should not be confused with a mortgage protection policy, which is a sensible precaution against your dying before the mortgage is paid off. The premiums are small and can be paid monthly or yearly, and your mortgage will be automatically settled upon your death. If both partners are earning and you have a joint mortgage, you can take out a joint mortgage protection policy which will pay out if either of you dies.

Buildings insurance

The buildings policy, or 'bricks and mortar' cover, insures the structure of the house, including fixtures and fittings, garages and outbuildings. There is also limited cover for boundary walls, fences, gates, paths and swimming pools. The normal cover is for damage caused by fire, thieves, water escaping from a damaged plumbing system, oil leaking from an oil-fired central heating system, storm, floods, rioters and malicious damage, explosion, lightning, impact of aircraft, vehicles or animals, falling trees, breakage or collapse of radio and TV aerials, earthquakes, subsidence or landslip. Impressive though this list is, there are exclusions, such as frost damage; moreover, the cover is not always comprehensive and will include 'excesses'. For example, 'storm and flood' damage does not apply to gates and fences; 'landslips and subsidence' excludes damage to outbuildings and paths; 'falling trees' does not include trees being felled or lopped. 'Excesses' means the exclusion of the first £15 of each claim; these usually apply to storm, flood and escape of water, impact and falling trees. The biggest excess is that on subsidence or landslip claims, where the first part of the claim is excluded – usually a proportion of the rebuilding cost amounting almost certainly to £250 or more.

It is the rebuilding costs of your home that you must consider when taking out buildings insurance. Do not insure at the market value of your home, unless it is a brand-new house, because building costs rise at a greater rate than house prices in most areas. Often the rebuilding costs for only partial damage can exceed the house's market value. Even if you are insuring a new house (at its market value *less* the land value) you should adjust the sum assured annually thereafter. Under-insuring property, according to the British Insurance Association, is a common failing with many householders. For first-time buyers it is an understandable failing: having poured all their savings into a mortgage, furniture and the like, they are also expected to pay for something that may never happen, so they try to cut the cost by taking out minimal insurance cover.

But disasters can happen, and do all too frequently. The number of houses totally destroyed by fire rises year by year (see Chapter Nine for ways of minimizing the risk) and building costs have increased by more than 200 per cent since 1965.

Estimating rebuilding costs

The problem is to get the sum assured just right – not too little, but not too much – which at one time meant either engaging a professional valuer, or trying to make an inspired guess. But since 1978 the Building Societies Association has recommended to its members that an insurance valuation should be carried out at the same time as the mortgage valuation. So all the home-buyer has to do is choose a good index-linked policy which will keep his sum assured up to date. Index-linking simply means that the sum assured and, of course, the premiums, are increased automatically whenever there is an upward move in building costs. One advantage of an index-linked policy is that although the sum assured is reviewed monthly the premium is not adjusted until the next renewal date. So for a short time in each period your home may be insured for more than you are actually paying in premiums. However, you must still inform the insurance company of any improvements to the house that will put up its rebuilding costs, such as the building of an extension or the installation of central heating.

If for some reason you have to make your own estimate of the insurance value (for example, if you are not borrowing from a building society) the British Insurance Association has published an excellent pamphlet called *A Guide to Buildings Insurance for the Home Owner*. It contains tables showing the estimated rebuilding costs for different types of dwelling of different ages and in various areas of the country. The figures are based on a report prepared by the Building Cost Information Service of the Royal Institute of Chartered Surveyors.

The tables show that older houses tend to cost more to rebuild than new ones; that bungalows have the highest rebuilding costs; and that for all types of property, London is dearest. A large, detached pre-war bungalow in the London area would cost about 25 per cent more to rebuild than a similar property in East Anglia. In estimating rebuilding costs, an allowance must be made for demolition costs, professional fees and local authority requirements, such as charges for the repair of damaged drains.

The BIA point out that the figures in their pamphlet are only a guide, and that costs can and do vary, depending upon individual circumstances. It is a good idea, therefore, to obtain an accurate figure for your area from a local builder or from the local branch of the Master Builders' Federation.

To arrive at a reasonably accurate insurance figure you simply find the total floor area of your house and multiply it by the rebuilding cost (£/ft^2).

To find the floor area, measure the length and breadth of the house on the outside. In the case of a semi-detached or a terraced house, measure on the inside of the party walls and add the wall thickness. Multiply the two figures together and you have the ground floor area in square feet. If the upstairs rooms are identical in size to those downstairs, simply double the ground floor figure to get the total floor area of the house. Otherwise you must measure the downstairs and upstairs floors separately and add the two together.

Assuming that the building costs quoted are £21 per square foot and the area of the house is 1,346 square feet, then the insurance value would be £28,266 (£21 x 1,346). To this should be added the estimated rebuilding costs of outbuildings, walls and fences. An attached garage should be included in the total area of the house.

Contents insurance

As we have seen, your loan source, or mortgagee, will insist that you insure the building, but no one will twist your arm when it comes to home contents insurance – except your insurance agent. Do not dismiss him as only being after more commission; insuring the contents of your home is just as important as insuring the house itself. The contents of a home, for insurance purposes, consist of just about everything you moved in with, plus whatever you have added since, including clothes, jewellery and money, as well as furniture and furnishings.

You can, if you wish, have a combined buildings and contents policy. It is well worth considering, for this type of policy often works out a little cheaper than having two separate policies. The cheapest type is the indemnity policy, in which the insurance company takes into account the wear and tear and depreciation in value of all items insured. Better cover is given by a reinstatement policy, where items stolen or damaged are replaced by new items. These 'new for old' policies are offered by most companies, but the amount of cover varies and it is worth shopping around to see which company gives the most comprehensive cover. Alternatively you can get a little of the best of both worlds with a mixed policy, which gives reinstatement cover on certain specified items and indemnity cover on the remainder.

Assessing the value of the contents

Working out the cover for household contents is a simple enough task, though it will require some checking of current prices. The best way to go about it is to go from room to room noting down the value of all the contents. For an indemnity policy, deduct an amount from each item for wear and tear. You can do this by deciding how much of its useful life an item has had: for example, a dining room suite could be expected to have a useful life of fifteen years, so if it is five years old deduct one-third from the current replacement price.

Antiques, works of art and jewellery need special care when it comes to assessing their value, as they invariably appreciate in value. Such items should be insured for the value a professional valuer would put on them; you should obtain a written valuation, so that if a claim has to be made it will be possible to prove to the insurer that the claim is reasonable.

A contents policy can be index-linked, with the cover adjusted monthly and no extra charge on the premiums between renewal dates. You must, however, increase your cover whenever you make an addition to your home contents. This, say the BIA, is where so many people become underinsured – they simply forget to increase their cover for the new colour TV, hi-fi, video-cassette player, etc.

The BIA have another leaflet, *Insurance for the Home Owner*, which includes a useful chart for estimating the total value of household goods. Room by room it lists such items as furniture, curtains and fittings and mentions expensive possessions that could easily be overlooked, such as cameras and binoculars. This leaflet and the guide to buildings insurance mentioned earlier are available free of charge from the British Insurance Association (see Appendix).

Insurance for tenants

If you are a tenant, and particularly if you are a single person in a small flat with few of your own possessions, you may consider insurance hardly worthwhile. But everybody has something of some value, and the majority of burglaries involve thefts of items worth less than £100. And even if you lose nothing of value in a burglary, the cost of the damage done by the intruder can be enormous.

Fire can do even more damage, and even a small fire quickly dealt with will produce enough smoke to ruin furnishings and decoration. If you are living in a flat you are also vulnerable to claims against you by other tenants (for example, if you leave a bath running and it overflows into the flat below). You are also responsible for any injury caused to a visitor, such as a fall caused by loose stair-carpet. It is not always realized that the tenant, not the landlord, is usually responsible for accidents of this sort.

In most cases the main risks are covered by the landlord's insurance, but there may be certain types of damage for which the tenant is responsible: for example, damage to washbasins and sanitary fittings and breakage of windows. Even where the tenant's liabilities are fairly limited, some types of damage, particularly that caused by smoke, can be very expensive to put right.

So even as a tenant, household contents insurance is advisable, and most insurance companies offer cover specifically tailored to tenants called 'Damage to Rented Premises' or 'Tenant's Liability'. The cover provided usually includes damage to buildings, interior decorations and landlord's fixtures and fittings, up to a maximum of 10 per cent of the sum insured for the contents. The first £15 of damage caused by storm, flood or burst pipes is sometimes excluded.

Also covered are the breakage of window glass and sanitary fittings and accidental damage to mains services such as water, gas and electricity.

If you have some of your own fixtures and fittings, such as fitted cupboards or wardrobe, these may be covered by the landlord's insurance. If not you may be able to have them included in your own insurance: ask your insurance agent, as practice varies from company to company.

In addition to the cover against damage to premises, household contents are insured in the same way for rented accommodation as for any household contents policy, and the types of cover available are the same, i.e. indemnity, reinstatement or mixed.

As is often the case elsewhere, in insurance you get what you pay for, and the wider the cover the higher the premiums. The amount of cover you require is something you must decide for yourself, but by paying a bit more you can acquire absolute peace of mind with an 'all-risks' policy. This covers items and eventualities not covered in a basic contents policy, such as a deep freezer and its contents, bicycles, loss of items outside the home and claims for damage caused by any member of the family.

Whatever insurance you have, remember that it is for your protection and should be used whenever the terms of the policy allow. It is foolish to under-insure, but it is equally foolish to pay high premiums year after year and get nothing in return. In almost every household, accidents occur which could be the subject of an insurance claim, a broken mirror or a scorched carpet, and many people forget or do not bother to claim.

Be insurance-conscious. Whenever something in your home is damaged – by accidental breakage, by fire or by flood – make it a habit to check the terms of your policy to see if you can make a claim. If you are not sure, ask your insurance agent.

9 Safe and Sound

'It's because she's so accident-prone that we bought this house.'

With good and ample insurance you can feel secure in your homes, knowing that whatever happens you will not suffer financially. But financial security cannot compensate for the misery caused by household disasters. Fire, burglary and accidents in the home are all, according to statistics, on the increase. It has been calculated that one in four people will be involved in a fire at some time during their lives. Even more frightening are the figures for burglary: it is said that people living in large towns are liable to be burgled at least twice in their lifetime. And deaths through accidents in the home equal those on the road, an average of eighteen per day, while one and a half million people are treated for injuries annually.

All these risks can be lessened considerably by the prudent householder – with a constant awareness of the dangers plus a few relatively cheap and simple precautions.

Awareness of the dangers is the most important of all the precautions for it would appear that householders are their own worst enemies. For example, Fire Prevention Officers say that there are three main causes of fire in the home – men, women and children. If you look around you it is not difficult to see how vulnerable homes are: the structure itself contains highly inflammable materials, and within the walls are furniture and furnishings that make the place a veritable tinder-box. Add to that the presence of electricity, gas and other fuels, and probably matches, and you have all the ingredients to start a raging inferno.

Electrical fires

Each room in the house has its own special dangers, but the risk common to all is electricity – the largest single cause of domestic fires, accounting for the destruction of some 20,000 homes each year.

In most houses, all the electrical wiring is concealed behind the plasterwork, where without anyone noticing the insulating sheathing can rot away or become impaired through overheating. Before moving into your home you will probably have had the wiring checked, if the previous owner had not had it done recently, and this is a good time to consider modifying the wiring system to safeguard against possible overloading in the future. It is a good idea to have extra power points fitted if necessary, so as to avoid the use of multi-way adaptors: these are a dangerous way of obtaining more power outlets, because using more than one appliance on a single socket outlet may cause overheating.

You can also have the main fuses replaced by circuit-breakers, which trip when the circuit is overloaded. You should, of course, have any electrical modifications carried out by qualified electricians. (From time to time the electricity boards run special offers for rewiring, the fitting of extra power points and the installation of circuit-breakers. Ask at your local electricity showroom.)

All electrical appliances, and their leads, should be serviced at least every two years by a qualified repairer, and especially electric blankets (these caused 8,000 fires during one recent winter). Electric blankets are made to a British Standard, BS 3456, and are perfectly safe if used properly. But the manufacturer's instructions should be followed carefully with regard to use and storage. Blankets intended for use under the bottom sheet should not be used as an over-blanket, and they should always be secured by the tapes provided so that the blanket will not crease and damage and elements. Similarly, care should be taken not to crease the blanket when storing it away for the summer.

Kitchen fires

Not surprisingly, about one-third of all house fires start in the kitchen, and usually at the cooker. The major cause of kitchen fires is a blazing frying-pan or deep-fryer. When cooking oil or fat is heated to a high temperature it becomes highly inflammable. A smoking pan or fryer is only seconds away from bursting into flames.

The worst aspect of a pan fire is the panic it often causes, which can lead to the fire being made worse. The rule, therefore, is to keep calm, turn off the heat under the pan and then cover the pan with a saucepan lid or a damp cloth. *Never* try to douse a pan fire with water as this will spread the burning fat, and never try to move the pan while it is still alight.

The design and layout of kitchen equipment and the decor are important in minimizing the fire risk. A wall cupboard above or close to the cooker may burn if a pan catches fire and the flames will quickly spread to adjacent units.

Electrical power points should be placed so that appliances such as kettles or coffee-makers cannot have their leads trailing across the cooker burners. Avoid the use of expanded polystyrene ceiling tiles in a kitchen, and certainly never use them above the cooker, because polystyrene melts rapidly when set alight and will drop burning fragments.

Inflammable furniture, window glass and decorating materials

The living room is the second most vulnerable room in the house. Contrary to general belief, most deaths in fires are not caused by burns but by suffocation. The living room usually contains more inflammable furnishings than any other room in the house, most of which give off choking and sometimes toxic fumes as they burn. Because living room fires usually start during the night when everyone is in bed, they have plenty of time to develop before spreading to the rest of the house. Often the fumes spread up the stairs and overcome the sleepers before they have a chance to escape.

Organizations concerned with domestic fires, such as the Fire Research Station and the Fire Protection Association, are alarmed at the increasing amount of highly inflammable materials used in modern furniture.

Plastics materials such as polyurethane, PVC, polypropylene, nylon, acrylics and polyesters burn fiercely, and a room filled with furniture incorporating these materials will be fully ablaze within five to seven minutes. Traditional materials – wood, wool, cloth, leather and horsehair, etc. – burn much more slowly, and in a room with all the doors and windows shut may burn for as long as five hours without becoming a serious hazard.

But modern materials are here to stay, and until the furniture manufacturers make their products fireproof, we can only take heed of the dangers and take extra care in rooms furnished with plastics-based furniture.

The use of bullion glass (the spun-glass panels used in Georgian-style bow windows and in decorative door panels) is another potentially dangerous modern trend. These very attractive and seemingly innocent reproductions of a traditional style have a built-in risk: they can concentrate the sun's rays like a magnifying glass and can start synthetic materials smouldering, particularly 'leather cloth' PVC. This type of glass should not be fitted where it is subject to direct sunlight, especially at mid-day. If this is unavoidable, it should be coated with a clear, acetate-based varnish that will give a rough finish and nullify the focusing effect.

The flammability of decorating materials should also be recognized as a potential fire hazard. Polystyrene, which is widely used because of its thermal insulation properties, is especially dangerous. Polystyrene sheeting and tiles should be fixed with an even layer of adhesive (heavyweight wallpaper paste is usually sufficient). Avoid using an occasional blob of fixative: this will allow air, which aids burning, to get behind the polystyrene.

If possible, always use non-flammable DIY materials. Some materials, such as paint strippers and impact adhesives, give off volatile fumes and should not be used in an unventilated room, or where a naked flame is present. Liquids such as cleaning fluids, paraffin and methylated spirits should be kept in a safe place where they cannot be knocked over, and not in the house if you have a garage or outside workshop.

Precautions against fire

Being sensible and taking simple precautions will considerably lower the risk of a fire breaking out in your home, but an element of risk is always present. Should a fire occur, the damage it causes can be kept to a minimum if you have taken the following two steps. The first is to fit smoke detectors: these are fitted to ceilings and will trigger off an alarm when smoke enters the unit. A low-powered battery is used to supply the current. The unit is thus independent of mains electricity, which may be cut off when a fire starts (especially if a short-circuit is the cause).

The second precaution is to have one or more fire extinguishers in the house. The powder-filled type are best for general use and can be used on both electrical and fat fires. The extinguisher should have a capacity of at least 2 lb (1 kg). Water can be used to deal with oil heater fires and burning fabrics or wood.

Tackling a fire

Tackle only small fires, and then only after ensuring that everyone is out of the house and after calling the fire brigade. Do not continue to fight a fire after it has obviously become out of control, and always make sure that your escape route is clear.

If you and your family become trapped in an upstairs room, close the door and block any cracks with bedding. Then try to rouse neighbours or passers-by with cries for help. If the situation becomes desperate, make a rope of sheets knotted together and tie one end to a bed leg. Alternatively, drop a mattress from the window, lower yourself from the windowsill and then drop feet first. Never jump from a window unless you have to.

Making the home secure against burglars

Every two minutes, someone's home, somewhere, is being robbed. Of the two main dangers in the home, burglary is probably the most unpleasant, because the damage an intruder can do has to be seen to be believed. Coming home to a house that has been burgled is an experience few people ever forget. For weeks, months and years the memory returns, and many people have been known to move because they could no longer live in a home that had been violated by some stranger.

People setting up home for the first time, and particularly newly-weds, are especially prone to an unwelcome visit. Obviously there will be many new items of value in the house – rich pickings for thieves who are on the look-out for people moving into new or otherwise empty property. And for the most part they rely entirely on the householder's carelessness in not locking up – often because they are only 'popping out' for a few minutes. But the majority of burglaries happen during the day, and a thief can clean out a house in as little as ninety seconds.

The majority of housebreakers are amateurs. 'Walk-in' opportunists account for 75 per cent of house robberies. They are easily deterred by fitting good, unpickable locks. Start with the front door, and if it has a spring lock (the type that clicks shut automatically) get rid of it and fit a deadlock, the type where you have to turn the key to lock it. Better still, fit a mortise deadlock which is built into the door and cannot be prised off with a jemmy. Chose a lock with at least five levers, and which carries the British Standards Kitemark. Fit a similar type of lock to the back door and to any other doors leading directly into the house.

Doors that open outwards, such as french windows, should be fitted with mortised bolts top and bottom. Hinge locks are also useful: they fit into the hinged side of the door so that it cannot be opened even if the bolts are forced.

Windows can be secured with special locks suited for any type of window. Fit them to all downstairs windows, and any upstairs that are near a drainpipe or above a convenient standing point, such as a porch or bay window.

If you have any doubts as to what precautions to take, contact your local Crime Prevention Officer. He will be pleased to advise you, free of charge, and a visit or phone call to the police station is all that is needed to arrange a visit.

Having made your home reasonably secure, get into the habit of locking up nightly before you turn in. When you go out, leave by the front door, *and take the key with you*. Never leave a key in a 'secret' hiding-place; however secret you think it may be, an experienced housebreaker will discover it in a matter of minutes.

If you have a garage or garden shed containing tools and ladders, fit a good-quality padlock. Do not leave ladders and tools around: most housebreakers can get in with nothing more than a screwdriver, so do not provide any extra help.

When you go on holiday, remember to cancel the milk and newspapers, or by the end of the first week it will as obvious that you are away as if you had put up a 'gone away' sign! One way of diverting attention from the fact that you are away, or out for a few hours at night, is to fit a time switch that will turn on an upstairs light in the evening and turn it off again later at about the time you normally go to bed. For good measure you could connect a radio to the switch as well.

Burglar alarms

If your home is likely to be left unattended for long periods, you may consider it worthwhile to fit a burglar alarm. There are a number on the market, and some systems include smoke detectors for fire protection. A sophisticated alarm system with pressure mats, sensors and smoke detectors can be quite expensive, but if you have valuables in the house, the money may be well spent. The National Supervisory Council for Intruder Alarms, a non-profitmaking body set up with Home Office approval, will give free advice (see Appendix).

Modern technology has come to the aid of home security, and there are now video systems available which enable to observe a caller at your front door on a TV screen. If you are out when someone calls, his or her image is recorded on video tape so that in the event of a break-in the intruder will have left visual evidence of their visit. Such a system would cost about £800 to install, but for most people the simple precaution of good locks on doors and windows is enough to deter the average burglar. If a potential housebreaker cannot gain entry within a few minutes he will move on, probably to a house where the owner has been less diligent.

Another danger for recent home-buyers is the bogus caller. Visits by representatives of gas, electricity, water and telephone companies are to be expected during the first few days after moving in, as the cunning thief well knows. The bogus 'official' may only be interested in having a few minutes alone so that he can pocket a few valuables, or he may be checking on the security and lay-out of the house for a later and more lucrative visit. Always ask for proof of identity if a caller claims to be on official business.

Falls in the home

In the time it has taken you to read this chapter, at least ten people will have been taken to hospital following an accident in the home, and probably at least one has died. That is a grim fact, especially in view of the fact that the home is surely the one place where we can consider ourselves safe. Ironically, it is because people relax in their homes that accidents occur: the major accidents are falls, resulting from sheer disregard of the dangers. The stairway and landing is probably the most hazardous part of the house. Never put off fixing a loose or worn carpet or an insecure hand-rail. Avoid the temptation to leave things at the foot of the stairs, ready to be taken upstairs the next time you are going that way. You will probably forget them on the way up, and may fall over them on the way down.

Stairways should be well-lit, with two-way switching upstairs and down. Any other parts of the house where there are dark corners or an awkward step should also have good lighting. It is a good idea to have a light outside the front and back doors, illuminating not only the doorstep but the path as well. Remember that you are liable for injuries to visitors on your premises if they are caused by your negligence.

Other hazards include highly-polished floors. If you must polish your floors, use the polish sparingly and make sure that all loose rugs have a non-slip backing. In your bathroom and kitchen mop up water spilled on the floor immediately: a minor fall in either room can be fatal if you hit your head on the hard edge of a washbasin or knock flying a saucepan of boiling water.

It seems that we are mostly likely to fall off kitchen stools and ladders, often through over-reaching to a shelf or cupboard. Step-ladders should always be locked in position and stood on an even surface. When using a ladder of any type make sure you have one hand free at all times. Take care, too, when cleaning windows: leaning out too far or sitting on the ledge of a sash-window frame can lead to a loss of balance and a fall. A fall from a downstairs window can result in bruises and sprains, while a fall from an upstairs window can be fatal. It is far better to employ a professional window-cleaner.

Electrical accidents

Treated with respect, electricity is a clean and efficient means of power; abused or neglected it is a deadly danger. It can be the silent and unseen enemy which, if neglected, can start fires, and it also represents the threat of electrocution.

Regular inspection of house wiring by a qualified electrician will ensure that the circuit is safe; the Institution of Electrical Engineers recommend inspection every five years. You can often see for yourself faults in appliances, such as frayed flexes, damaged plugs and sockets or broken switches. Such faults should be put right as soon as they are spotted. When fitting a new plug, remember the colour coding: brown to live, blue to neutral, yellow-green to earth. Most plugs are sold with a 13-amp fuse, but this may be too high a rating for some appliances. Generally, appliances rated at 700 watts or more need a 13-amp fuse, but below 700 watts a 3-amp fuse should be fitted. If you are not sure of the power rating of an appliance, ask at your local electricity showroom or contact the manufacturer.

Electricity shares your house with a dangerous neighbour – water. Keep them apart at all times: never take an electrical appliance into a bathroom and on no account touch or pick up an appliance with wet hands; do not fill an electric kettle or coffee percolator when in it is plugged in; do not use an iron in the kitchen when the floor is damp. Never take chances with electricity.

First aid

However careful you are, accidents will happen – though not often and not serious ones if you take sensible precautions. Every household should have a first-aid box stocked with plasters, bandages, and treatments for minor burns, cuts, bruises, etc. Make sure the box is easy to get at in an emergency, and that everyone in the house knows where it is.

If someone is involved in a serious accident, such as a bad fall, severe burning or electrocution, send for an ambulance at once. Then apply what first aid you can, depending on the symptoms. An unconscious victim should be kept on his side with face turned towards the ground. Loosen clothing at the neck, chest and waist and ensure that the victim is breathing freely. Never try to revive a casualty with drinks, such as brandy, while he is still unconscious, and do not give him a drink of any kind if injury to the lungs or abdomen is suspected, or if an anaesthetic is likely to be needed.

Do not try to move a casualty unless you are certain what is wrong, and even then only if you have to; it is better to keep the victim warm and comfortable until help arrives.

It is a sad reflection of our times that the more comfortable and easy to run our homes become, the greater is the risk of accidents. This chapter has dealt with only the tip of a horrifying iceberg, and all householders are recommended to acquaint themselves fully with all the risks. The police, hospitals, doctors and libraries can supply books and pamphlets on safety in the home, and the Royal Society for the Prevention of Accidents has a useful booklet called *Safe as Houses?*, obtainable from ROSPA, Cannon House, The Priory Queensway, Birmingham.

10 The Castle Syndrome

'It's just as well mother's a policewoman, otherwise you'd never let her come and visit.'

There is probably no more familiar saying than 'an Englishman's home is his castle'. To a certain extent the law supports this view, but it also permits many people to enter your home, with or without your permission and often with the right to use force.

It is estimated that some 10,000 civil servants and local government employees are entitled to enter private premises; add to that the police, main service officials (from the gas, water and electricity boards), landlords and bailiffs and your 'castle walls' begin to look rather fragile.

Even trespassers enjoy a measure of protection: you are limited in the amount of force you can use in dealing with them and can find yourself on a charge of assault if you use more force than the law allows.

You are expected to act as a responsible, law-abiding citizen even behind your own front door - a reasonable demand as long as you know what the law requires of you, but do you? Are you fully aware of who may lawfully demand entry to your home, and under what circumstances? When you take a driving test, the law requires that you are acquainted with the rules of the Highway Code, but there is no 'Householder's Code' telling you what you can and cannot do when you take on one of the biggest responsibilities of all - running a home.

Authorized intruders

As a law-abiding citizen you are seldom likely to have your home invaded by officialdom, but it is essential that you should know exactly where you stand when someone demands entry. Refusing entry to someone who has a legal right to demand it may get you into even more trouble; but there is no need to allow anyone to enter who has no right to do so.

Council officials may enter private homes on matters connected with public health. They are authorized by the Public Health Acts, which deal with such matters as pest and vermin control and infectious diseases. The Housing and Planning Acts also permit officials to enter to deal with overcrowding, demolition orders and slum clearance. In all cases the official must have written authorization from the council, which the householder can demand to see, otherwise he can be refused entry.

Gas and electricity board officials may, of course, enter your home to read meters, repair faults and inspect fittings, all of which they do with your permission, but you may and should ask them for evidence that they are employed by the board concerned. They may also enter to cut off the supply, which will not be much to your liking but you may not refuse entry. Both gas and electricity officials can obtain warrants allowing them to use reasonable force to get in, and a householder who refuses entry to an authorized official is liable to a fine.

Water authorities have similar rights, but they have the added advantage over the householders in that they can cut off the supply outside the house if entry is refused. They, also, may use force if they come armed with a magistrate's warrant.

Post Office engineers have the right to inspect or remove telephones, but cannot obtain a warrant to enter. Instead the PO may sue for return of its property. TV detector-van engineers may enter if their records show that you are operating a TV set without a licence. If refused entry they can obtain a magistrate's warrant and can also ask a policeman to accompany them if they have reason to believe that there may be a breach of the peace.

Anyone suspected of keeping contraband may receive a visit from Customs and Excise officials, who carry a High Court search warrant (called a Writ of Assistance) allowing them to force entry and to break open containers which may hold illicit goods.

The rights of the police

The police may not normally force their way into your home without your permission or a warrant, unless they are trying to prevent a breach of the peace or intend to make an arrest. They can, however, search premises occupied by someone who has been convicted of theft or receiving stolen goods within the past five years, and for this they need only the written authority of a police superintendent. The police may enact any of their powers at any time of the day or night, and without prior warning.

A police superintendent may also give written authority for his officers to search premises if he has reasonable grounds for believing that an offence is being committed with respect to explosives, and that delay in searching is likely to endanger life. He may take similar action if, in his opinion, persons or places should be searched for evidence of an offence under the Official Secrets Act.

Without a warrant, the police may enter your home only with your permission, which they may gain by a remark such as, 'May I come in, Sir? I'm sure you don't want the whole street watching me standing on your doorstep.' This invocation of the fear of gossip seldom fails. He may then suggest casually that he has 'a quick look round' while he is there. Having allowed him to enter you cannot complain of his presence, or to his searching the premises if you have not objected to his suggestion. But you may withdraw your permission at any time, in which case the policeman then becomes a trespasser and may be ejected.

One instance of police trespass has resulted in a House of Lords ruling. This was when the police pursued a motorist for the purpose of demanding a breath test and entered his home. The motorist refused to take a breath test in his own house and was arrested, but the House of Lords ruled that the police were trespassing and had no right to enter someone's home for that purpose. Most officials other than the police may demand entry only during reasonable hours, although gas and electricity officials may enter at any time if they have reason to believe that life or property is in danger.

The warrant which grants officials the right to enter your home is issued by a magistrate: you, the householder, are not notified that a warrant is being applied for, nor are you permitted to oppose it. There would be little point, anyway, for the issue of a warrant is a mere formality. The person applying for the warrant already has the right, under the law, to enter private premises: the issue of a warrant confirms that right.

Bailiffs and sheriffs

One group of officials with wide powers is the bailiffs of the County Courts, who carry out court orders to seize goods in order to settle debts. They may enter your home during the day or night (except on Sunday) but may only do so through an unlocked door or open window. Bailiffs can also seize hire-purchase property for re-possession, using a Warrant for Delivery, and may use force, if necessary, to enter. They may also use force to evict a tenant under a Warrant for Possession, though only during reasonable hours.

Orders made by a High Court are carried out by Sheriff's officers who have similar rights and powers to those of bailiffs. Should you be unfortunate enough to receive a visit from either, you must remember that they are carrying out court orders: resistance constitutes contempt of court.

Fortunately, bailiffs are no longer the moustache-twirling villains of Victorian melodrama and are limited in what goods they can seize. They are not allowed to take essential goods such as bedding and clothing, though a mink coat could be an exception! They must also leave any tools or books of your trade not exceeding a total value of £50. Goods which are acquired under a hire-purchase agreement may not be taken, unless they are being re-possessed, because they are the property of the hirer until the final payment has been made.

There is another type of bailiff, called Certificated Bailiffs; these are private companies employed to seize goods in order to pay taxes, rents and rates. They are licensed to operate under the laws of distress, and the process is known as distraint. Their certificate is granted by a magistrate or by the registrar of a county court. Like court bailiffs and sheriffs, certificated bailiffs are not allowed to operate on Sundays, and they may enter your home only between sunrise and sunset. They are not allowed to force an entry under any circumstances.

Valuation Officers

If you have improved or enlarged your home, thus making yourself liable for higher rates, you may get a visit from a Valuation Officer of the Inland Revenue. He, too, may not use force to gain entry, but you are liable to a fine if you obstruct him. Valuation Officers must make their visits during reasonable hours, and must give at least 24 hours' warning.

A visit from a bailiff or sheriff's officer can be an alarming experience, but you should always challenge their right to enter by demanding to see written evidence of their authority. This may be a court order, a judgement summons, a distress warrant, a warrant for delivery or writ of delivery, a warrant for possession or writ of possession. If you have not been aware that an application to the court has been made, you may ask the bailiff for a 48-hour respite, so that you can consult a solicitor. Though not obliged to do so, a bailiff will usually agree.

Your neighbours' rights

Even your neighbour has the right to enter your home – to repair or examine common walls or shared services. But he may not use force, nor will the police assist him, and his only recourse is to take action through the courts if you persist in denying him access.

You have responsibilities to your neighbours, particularly with regard to not creating a nuisance. Your neighbour may apply to a court for an order, known as an injunction, to make you stop doing whatever it is that is annoying him, but only if you have acted unreasonably. For example, your neighbour may complain about a particularly noisy party, and may even call the police. But unless you are holding wild parties habitually there is little he can do, and the police will take no action other than suggesting to you that you act in a more neighbourly fashion.

A group of neighbours acting together can apply to the local authority to serve a notice on you to stop any noise which amounts to a nuisance, if the noise is persistent and more than anyone can be reasonably expected to tolerate. The court will not intervene, however, if the noise is caused by you or one of your family learning to play a musical instrument, however excruciating it may be. But the court will certainly act if it can be shown that you are making a noise deliberately to annoy your neighbour, even if the noise itself is not excessive.

Nuisance can also be caused by offensive smells, which also must be persistent to give grounds for action. The smoke and smell of an occasional garden bonfire may be annoying, but it is no more an acceptable cause for action than is the occasional noisy party.

How to deal with trespassers and burglars

The law gives you the right to protect your property and to keep out intruders by putting up some kind of defences, such as barbed wire or broken glass embedded in the top of a wall. But such deterrents should be visible, and you are not allowed to plant booby traps or any devices that could kill or maim an intruder.

You are allowed to keep a fierce dog: but it is best that his bark is worse than his bite, because if he cannot tell the difference between a housebreaker and the gas-meter reader you may soon be in trouble.

It is not advisable to display a 'Beware of the Dog' sign, since this is evidence of the fact that you know the dog is dangerous and therefore you may be liable if it bites someone.

When dealing with trespassers, any force you use must be 'reasonable' and in proportion to the degree of danger in which you consider yourself to be, but in a tense and heated situation few people would be able to make a rational assessment, and the householder who over-reacts may find himself in court instead of the trespasser.

If someone breaks into your home at night, the law will take a different view and you may counter violence in kind. For example, if a burglar threatens you with a gun you may shoot him. You may also use any weapon that comes to hand, such as a walking stick or a piece of wood, even if the intruder is unarmed but threatens to attack you physically. It is inadvisable, however, to tackle an intruder alone unless you have to. If you are awakened at night by the sound of someone in your home, try to get out of the house unobserved and phone the police from a call box or from a neighbour's house. There is a much better chance of the burglar being caught if the police arrive while he is still on the premises, but if you scare him off yourself he may still get away with valuables.

Visitors' and tradesmen's rights

Anyone who visits your home, either at your invitation or by legal right, may sue you for damages if he or she suffers injury caused by your negligence. It could be a postman who slips and falls on an icy path, an electricity meter-reader who receives a shock through faulty wiring, or your maiden aunt who trips over a hole in the carpet. They may not, however, take action if they have been warned of the danger, or if the accident occurs in a part of the house in which they have no right to be.

Workmen are expected to be aware of any dangers connected wth their trade; if you hire someone to erect a TV aerial it is his own fault if he falls off the roof. But if he falls through the roof because of a structural weakness in it, you are responsible and he may sue you even if you had warned him of the danger.

If this chapter has alarmed you, be assured that in a well-run home the occurrences described will seldom, if ever, arise. Trouble with neighbours can be avoided simply by being reasonable and considerate; burglars and trespassers can be kept out by applying the measures described in Chapter Nine. As for the bailiffs, and any other officials demanding their pound of flesh, take a look at Chapter Eleven to find out how to keep them away.

11 The Costs of Being a Householder

Though your home may not be a castle, at least you are the king within it, and as sovereign you are responsible for the treasury. Unlike the king of the nursery rhyme, however, most of your time will be spent counting the money that goes out, and if you are to avoid visits from some of the gentlemen mentioned in Chapter Ten, you must be sure that your financial commitments are fully met, and on time.

A large part of the household outgoings must, of course, be on food, drink, items for the house and other incidentals. You can keep down such costs by careful housekeeping and by living within your means; when prices rise and push up the housekeeping bill you have either to do without something or dip deeper into your income. The choice is yours, but there are some costs over which you have little or no control: for example, you must have lighting and heating, and although you can economize on these essentials there is a limit to what you can do without making your life miserable. There are other items, too, which though not essentials you may wish to have, such as a colour television and a telephone. So the bills must be paid, and if you organize your budget efficiently you can avoid the embarrassment of being faced with several heavy commitments at a time when you can least afford them.

Rates

Before looking at ways of keeping the bailiffs from the door, you must consider the one commitment which, as a householder, you can never avoid: rates, a tax levied on all owners or occupiers of property in order to pay for education, welfare services, street cleaning, refuse collection, sewerage, and so on.

How rates are assessed

What you pay in rates depends on two factors: the rateable value of your property and a proportion of that value levied by the local council, known as the 'rate in the pound'. The rateable value is assessed by the Inland Revenue Valuation Office, which sends a questionnaire to the occupier which he must complete truthfully and return within twenty-one days. From this information, and in conjunction with a survey of the property, the valuation officer calculates what yearly rent could be charged if you were to let the property. This figure is called the 'gross value', and from it a percentage is deducted which allows for the costs of maintenance and repairs and insurance. The net figure is the rateable value.

If you are a tenant, you may find that a portion of your rent goes towards the rates, but you are still liable if your rent is 'exclusive of rates'. The 'rate in the pound' is fixed by the local council, either yearly or half-yearly, and rate demands are sent out to all ratepayers. If, for example, the rate is 80p in the pound, then the demand for rates on property with a rateable value of £100 would be £80. Rates are payable in advance, but can be paid in twice-yearly instalments or, in many cases, in monthly instalments.

Paying your rates

Rate demands must be paid within a period of seven days, after which the local council can apply for a summons for the defaulter to appear in a magistrates' court. If no valid reason is given for non-payment of the rates, or a promise to pay is not made in court, then a distress warrant may be issued as described in Chapter Ten. After seizure of goods by a bailiff, five days are allowed during which the rates demand can be settled, but if it is not the goods will be sold to retrieve the debt. If the value of the seized goods is insufficient to cover the debt, the court can impose a prison sentence of up to three months.

So, paying your rates must come high on the list of priorities in the household budget in view of the dire consequences of non-payment; it is as important an obligation as mortgage or rent payments. If it is possible to pay by monthly instalment, you may find it preferable to pay in this way, either by a standing order with your bank or by direct debiting. Otherwise a set amount should be saved each month, in a good savings bank, ready for the time when the rates demand arrives.

Obtaining a rates reduction

It is sometimes possible to obtain a reduction in your rates, either by appealing against the rateable value assessment or by applying for a rates rebate. An appeal for re-assessment can be made if you consider that the property could not be let at the figure arrived at by the valuation officer. There may be factors that the valuation officer has not taken into account, or perhaps was not aware of, or circumstances may have changed since the last valuation: for example, a factory might have been built next door.

A form called 'Proposal for the Alteration of the Valuation List', available from the local valuation office, is used to register the appeal. You must outline fully the reasons for the objection, and though you are not required to suggest a fair rateable value it is a good idea to do so. Your case will be considerably strengthened if there are other householders in your neighbourhood who also consider their rateable value to be excessive, and are prepared to form a group and engage a lawyer to handle the appeal.

The appeal goes before a valuation court, at which documents and witnesses can be produced in support of the case. The court's decision need not be final; if you are dissatisfied you can appeal to the Lands Tribunal. At this stage, however, you would certainly need professional advice and you should consider the cost against what you hope to achieve. It is unlikely that you will obtain a big enough **reduction in your rateable value to warrant lawyers' and perhaps surveyors' fees.**

All ratepayers, whether owner or tenant, can obtain a rates rebate if they can show that they are unable to pay the full amount without suffering hardship. It is usually people with low incomes who gain rates rebates; but you do not have to be on the bread line to obtain a reduction, and in some areas where the rates are very high it is possible for someone earning more than £10,000 a year to get a rebate. Tenants whose rates are included in their rent can also qualify for a rebate.

Application must be made on a form obtainable from the local council treasurer's office, and confidential details will be required such as your employer's name and address, your gross income and spouse's gross income where applicable, as well as details of any income from other sources. Before applying, however, you should seek the advice of the local rates office or Citizens' Advice Bureau, who will be able to tell you if your application is likely to be successful.

In addition to the general rate you also have to pay water rates, levied either by the council or by a water authority. Sometimes the water rate is a percentage of the rateable value, or it may be a 'rate in the pound'. Water rates usually become due half-yearly or quarterly and are not payable by monthly instalments. Nor is a rates rebate possible. If the water rate is not paid, the water may be cut off outside the house and the ratepayer will have to pay both the costs of disconnecting and reconnecting the supply as well as his rate arrears.

Budgeting for bills

Bills have a nasty habit of arriving in batches, and at the worst possible time. There is nothing more calculated to spoil a holiday homecoming than finding a pile of official-looking envelopes on the mat, especially if any of them are final demands. And in the weeks immediately following Christmas, the season of goodwill seems to evaporate rapidly in accounts offices throughout the land.

Many of those communications, however, could be merely for information – statements which show your current position in a budget payment scheme. This method of payment is particularly useful for gas and electricity; your annual consumption of gas or electrical units is estimated and you then pay monthly, by standing order, an amount specified by the accounts department of the supplier. During the winter months when consumption of gas and electricity is high, your quarterly statement may show you as being in arrears, but you are not required to make up the balance as this should be automatically redressed during the summer. If your monthly payments have been over-estimated, so that your statements throughout the year show you as being constantly in credit, you will get a refund and a revised payment total. More likely, however, you will receive from time to time a revised payment figure which allows for price increases.

On a much wider scale, you can pay almost all your regular bills with a budget account at your bank. This is how it works: you add up all the bills you expect to receive in the coming year - rates, telephone, gas, electricity, insurances, licences, annual subscriptions, etc. - and then divide the total by twelve. You then pay that amount monthly into your current account, which the bank then transfers to a budget account. From the time the first transfer is made you can write out cheques to pay the bills as they come in, on special budget cheques provided by the bank, though you are asked not to make a single payment which exceeds one-quarter of the total commitment.

By using a budget account you can ensure that all bills are paid in full and on time, but you have to pay for this peace of mind. The charge is usually £20 for the first £500 of your total commitment, and then £1 for every £50 or part of £50 after that. There is no charge, however, for budget payment schemes with the gas and electricity boards, and you can apply to use this method of payment at the accounts office in your local showrooms.

Direct debiting

A good way of paying bills which vary either in the amount or in the interval between them is by direct debiting. As for a standing order, you give your bank instructions to meet certain payments as they fall due, but with direct debiting the firm or organization to whom payment is owed presents the bill, and the bank deducts that amount from your account. There are two methods of direct debiting: one deals with payment of fixed amounts and the other provides for payment of amounts that vary.

Direct debiting is useful for paying yearly subscriptions and fees that increase by an unspecified amount each year: payment is made only on your authorization and the organization or firm concerned must notify you in advance of the amount and date of the payment. The bank offers a safeguard against unauthorized debiting; it will reimburse you if a direct debit is made which does not conform to your instructions.

One organization now using direct debiting is the National Television Licence Records Office, but if you would rather have closer control over saving for a TV licence you can buy special savings stamps issued by the Post Office. You can also save for telephone bills in this way: cards on which you stick the stamps are available at any post office.

Credit schemes

If you want to buy goods on credit, such as furniture, kitchen appliances, carpets or a car, you can do so either by a hire-purchase agreement or by a credit-sale agreement. The major difference between the two methods is that in a hire-purchase agreement the goods belong to the hire-purchase company until the last instalment is paid, whereas the customer becomes the owner from the outset in a credit-sale agreement. Either way, interest is paid to the hirer or creditor.

The amount of deposit required for a hire purchase transaction, and the period of time in which the loan must be paid off, is controlled by government regulations.

Undoubtedly the best way to get short-term credit is with a credit card such as Access or Barclaycard. You can use the card to make purchases in stores that will accept the card, and if you pay off your debt each month the credit is free. One advantage of a credit card is that you can settle all your debts on one cheque.

Many stores and supermarkets operate their own credit schemes, and there are two common types. In one, known as a budget or subscription account, the store allows you to spend up to a certain limit based on how much you can afford to repay each month. As you pay off your debt you can continue to spend providing you do not go over your limit. The other type of credit scheme, called an option account, works in much the same way as a bank credit card. Interest is payable on both of these schemes, however.

Whenever you buy anything on credit you should make sure you know how much the credit charge will be. Here the law has come to the aid of the consumer. All credit traders must now calculate their interest and credit charges in a standard way, and show them as the 'APR'. This stands for 'Annual Percentage Rate of the Total Charge for Credit', and you will see it displayed either on the goods or in the trader's advertisements. The APR, shown as a percentage, tells you the full amount of interest you will have to pay and thus helps you shop around for the best credit buy.

The obligation on traders to display the APR is a provision of the Consumer Credit Act, and it protects consumers in other ways too. For example, if something is wrong with the goods or service bought on credit, both the vendor and the creditor are responsible for putting matters right. In such a case you should contact the creditor immediately as well as the supplier. If you think your credit charges are too high you can go to court and ask for a reduction. But you should be very sure you have a good case, and as a first step contact the local Trading Standards Department, Citizens' Advice Bureau or a Consumer Advice Centre. Their advice is free.

Bank loans

Another way of obtaining credit is through your bank, by taking a personal loan, though on some items such as cars and furniture the loan is subject to the government's hire-purchase regulations. Your bank manager will advise you of any such conditions. One advantage of borrowing from your bank is that the debt is cancelled in the event of your death before the loan is repaid.

It is wise to make full use of bank facilities and credit systems. By using standing orders, direct debiting and a budget account you can be sure that the bills will be paid; personal loans and credit buying will help you improve your living standards quickly, providing you are prudent and do not succumb to the temptations of easy buying. A good maxim to remember is Mr Micawber's observation: 'Annual income twenty pounds, annual expenditure nineteen nineteen six, result happiness. Annual income twenty pounds, annual expenditure twenty pounds ought and six, result misery.'

Gas tariffs

When you move into your home, one of the first things you must decide is which gas and electricity tariffs will suit you best. Gas tariffs are fairly straightforward. There are only two that concern domestic supplies: the credit tariff and the prepayment tariff. As its name implies, you pay for gas on the credit tariff after you have used it. Your meter is read quarterly and you pay two charges: a standing charge (£8.00

per quarter in 1981), and a commodity charge at 27.2p per therm.

The prepayment tariff is a 'pay-as-you-go' method, for which you are provided with a coin-in-the-slot meter. Prepayment gas is charged at 43.0p per quarter for the first 39 therms and further therms are charged at 29.2p. The standing charge is £3.00 (at time of going to press). A prepayment slot meter will be fitted only where it is safe and practical to do so, and is only more advantageous than the credit method where gas consumption is small, such as through a cooker only or one small cooker and one gas fire.

If you are living in a small flat, the landlord may install a 'check' meter and require you to pay for gas separately. This is perfectly legal providing that the landlord does not charge you at a higher rate than the maximum resale charge laid down by the Gas Acts. Details of these charges can be obtained from your local gas showrooms.

If no one is at home when the meter reader calls to read your credit meter your next bill will be estimated, based on previous readings. But if you do not agree with the estimate you can read the meter yourself, fill in the dials or boxes on the back of the bill and return it to the gas office. To read the meter, look at the lower row of four dials and read from left to right. Where the hand is between two figures, take the lower one except where it is between '9' and '0', in which case put down '9'.

You can also read your meter from time to time to keep a regular check on the amount of gas you are using. Subtract the figures of your last bill from the new reading and this will give you the amount of gas used in hundreds of cubic feet. Gas is charged by the therm, which is a unit of heat. To convert the figure in cubic feet to therms, first find the calorific value (CV) which is shown on your gas bill. Then make the calculation using the formula 'calorific value x hundreds of cubic feet ÷ 1000 = therms'. For example, gas supplied at a calorific value of 1035 with a consumption of 28 hundred cubic feet would be 1035 x 28 divided by 1000 = 29 therms (approximately).

To get some idea of what various gas appliances cost to run, here are some average consumption figures for one year: gas cooker, 80 therms; main living room fire, 200 therms;

separate hot-water supply, 210 therms. Gas central heating in a small house or flat will use about 750 therms; in a medium-sized semi-detached house about 860 therms; and in a large detached house about 1,265 therms.

Electricity tariffs

The Electricity Board offers four domestic tariffs. Most homes are supplied under the Standard Domestic Rate, with a standing charge of 45p per week and a unit charge of 4.44p (1982). If, however, you use a fair amount of electricity at night there are two 'Night and Day' rates available: Night and Day Rate 1 offers cheaper 'off-peak' units during the ten hours of the night period, but the standing charge is 58p per week and the day unit charge is 4.86p. The charge for night units is 2.56p. Night and Day Rate 2, also called Economy Seven, has a seven-hour night period in which units are charged at 1.82p. The day unit charge is 4.74p and the standing charge 58p per week. Night and Day rates are useful if you have night storage heaters and/or electrical water heating.

The fourth tariff is a 'pay-as-you-go' slot-meter rate, with a standing charge of 64p per week and units charged at 4.44p. As for gas, this method is advisable only if your electricity consumption is small. It cannot be used if you have electrical central heating, nor is it advisable if you have a refrigerator or a freezer.

Your local electricity office will advise you on which tariff is best suited to your needs, but it is helpful to know what sort of current consumption various appliances use. An electrical unit is consumed by using electricity at the rate of 1 kilowatt (1000 watts) for one hour. So, for example, a 100-watt lamp will consume one unit in ten hours; a 250-watt appliance will use one unit in four hours; and a 1-kilowatt heater will burn up one unit in one hour.

Some other examples are: colour TV, 6 hours per unit; stereo stystem, 8-10 hours per unit; tumble dryer, 30 minutes per unit; vacuum cleaner, 2 hours per unit. It is difficult to assess the amount of current consumed by electrical central heating as there are several different types, but the average yearly consumption for a warm air system is said to be about

1700 units for every kilowatt (kW) of the calculated heat requirement. A 5 kW requirement, for example, will consume about 8,500 units during a 32-week heating season. A 2 kW storage-heater system uses between 1800 and 2400 units during the same period.

The price of solid fuel and oil

Solid fuel and oil prices vary from dealer to dealer, so it is wise to shop around for coal, coke or paraffin. Often you can get a reduction by paying promptly (at the time of ordering or on delivery) and you can sometimes obtain reduced rates for large deliveries. If you are using solid fuel for water heating or central heating, make sure you are using the most suitable fuel. Advice is available from the Solid Fuel Advisory Service (see Appendix).

12 Improving Your Home

'We've doubled the size of the kitchen by knocking down the wall into the coal store.'

When you look for a home, you are likely to find that what you want and what you can afford seldom coincide. So you will probably end up with a compromise, having sacrificed some of your requirements in order to stay within a price range. But once you have made your choice and have settled into your home, with all the initial costs out of the way, you can then consider making a start on a range of improvements that will bring it up to the standard you desire.

There are many worthwhile improvements that can be made to a home to provide more space or more comfort. They will increase the value of the property, but may consequently lead to an increase in the rateable value. So you should consider how essential an improvement is, and whether you are prepared to pay extra rates for it, before embarking on any major projects.

One improvement, however, which does not lead to an immediate revaluation is central heating. Since 1974, no increase in the rateable value has been levied on new central heating installations until the next general revaluation. If you are planning to install central heating, find out when the next general revaluation is due: it may be worth waiting a year or two in order to take advantage of a long period – at least five years – when your rates will not be affected.

Central heating systems

Central heating has come to be regarded as an essential rather than a luxury. There are few dwellings, old or new, that cannot be fitted with one of the various systems available. A widely used system employs the 'wet' principle, in which water heated by a central boiler is pumped to radiators situated around the house. The boiler may be heated by gas, oil or solid fuel. There is also an electrical warm-air system, Electricaire, in which air is heated and then blown through ducts by electrically operated fans. Floor and ceiling heating systems are also available, but all these electrical systems are suitable only for building into a new house or one that is undergoing extensive modernization. There are also storage heaters, running on off-peak electricity, though these are not, strictly speaking, central heating because each radiator is a heat source in itself.

In most modern central heating systems the hot-water supply for kitchen and bathroom taps is also heated, and is separate from the water circulating in the radiators.

When deciding which type of system to use (gas, oil, solid fuel or electricity), the most important factors to consider are the installation cost and running costs. Choosing which fuel to use is difficult, since fuel costs never stay constant for long. At one time, oil-fired systems were very popular, but when oil prices rose dramatically many people changed to gas, which has itself now risen in price but is still cheaper than oil.

Deciding which fuel to use involves a careful study of current fuel prices, running costs and a crystal ball. Generally, gas-fired systems and electrical heating have two advantages over oil and solid fuel: oil and solid fuel have to be stored on the premises and are sometimes subject to shortages caused by strikes or international incidents. Gas-fired systems have an advantage over electrical heating in that gas supplies are not prone to power cuts. In some rural areas, however, there is no mains gas supply, so gas may not be a viable alternative.

The cost of a gas-fired installation will depend on the size of the house and the number of rooms to be heated, but you can expect to pay at least £1,000 for a system in a medium-sized semi-detached house. The running costs, however, when compared with the cost of heating each room separately and heating the hot-water supply, make central heating worthwhile. A gas-fired boiler heating the water supply and six radiators will cost only about 25 per cent more than it would to heat a single room with a gas fire and the hot water from a separate boiler.

Storage heaters

Storage heaters can be a good alternative to central heating. One advantage is that while all the heat from a storage heater goes into the room, about 25 per cent of the heat from a boiler goes up the flue. It is also claimed that storage heaters are cheaper to install than a full central heating system – less than £1,000 for a medium-sized semi – and no pipes or flues are needed.

There are four types of storage heater: damper-controlled heaters, which can be made to release their heat at a greater rate at the end of the day by either manual or automatic controls; the static heater, which is a simple unit controlled by an input charge controller; fan-assisted heaters, which release more heat at the end of the day by means of a fan, and the storage fan heater, which has a fan controlled by a thermostat and distributes warm air in the room when required. Other types of electrical heaters can be used in conjunction with storage heaters, especially in rooms where heat is not needed at all times. A suggested all-electric layout is: hall, storage heater; living room, storage heater and electric fire; dining room, storage heater or radiant fire; bedroom, panel heater with thermostat; spare bedroom, convector heater; bathroom, radiant heater or wall-mounted fan heater and heated towel-rail.

It is claimed that electrical central heating needs no maintenance, and the Solid Fuel Advisory Service say that cleaning the chimney or flue once a year is all the servicing required by solid-fuel systems. Gas and oil systems, however, should be regularly serviced and it is worthwhile paying for a maintenance and servicing scheme, as offered by British Gas and by various oil distributors.

Insulating the home

The economical use of central heating depends on the use of proper controls and good insulation. A thermostat should be fitted to control the overall temperature, and some radiators can be controlled individually with thermostatic valves. It is essential, too, to fit a time switch so that the system is automatically switched off when the house is empty, and at night when the heat is not needed.

Insulation should begin at the hot water cylinder, which should be fitted with a thermal jacket to hold the heat in. Similarly, all pipes leading to the radiators should be lagged so that heat is not wasted in areas such as under the floor and in cupboards. Pipe lagging material and thermal jackets can be bought at most DIY shops (the British Standard for thermal jackets is BS 5615).

The most effective way to keep down heating costs is to insulate the house itself. This is a valuable improvement whatever form of heating is used, because much of that heat escapes through the roof, walls and windows.

About 25 per cent of the total heat loss is through the roof. There are two methods of roof insulation which are well within the scope of the average handyman. One widely used method is to lay rolls of glass-fibre between the ceiling joists in the roof space. The rolls are available in thicknesses of 3 or

4 inches, but the 4-inch thickness is the most effective at little more cost. If your loft is an awkward shape, making it difficult to lay the glass-fibre rolls, you can use vermiculite pellets. These should be spread evenly between the joists to a depth of at least three inches.

You can defray the cost of insulating your loft, either in part or in full, by getting a grant from your local council. The grant is £69 or 66 per cent of the total cost, whichever is the smaller amount. There are conditions to be met, however, and one is that the loft has not been insulated before – even if it has been done very badly. Another condition is that you use approved materials (your local council office will have a list) and that they are laid to the required depth.

Most post-war houses have cavity walls, which give a measure of insulation that can be further improved by filling the cavity with a special foam, polystyrene pellets or mineral wool.

Filling cavity walls is a job for experts. Should you decide to have it done go to a specialist firm recognized by the National Cavity Insulation Association. A number of 'cowboy' firms have sprung up in this field, and reports that cavity filling allows damp to penetrate from the outer wall to the inner wall are due almost entirely to inferior grades of foam being used by amateurs.

If your home is one of the older solid-wall designs, there is little you can do other than to clad the inside of the walls with insulating panels, or apply rolls of thin polystyrene sheeting to the walls before papering. There are exterior insulating methods available, in which polystyrene panels are fitted to the walls and then covered with rendering, but again this is a job for specialists and can be expensive (about £1,500 for a medium-sized semi-detached house).

Double glazing

Heat loss through windows can be reduced by double glazing, but it should be stressed that windows account for only about 10 per cent of the total heat loss, and double glazing is only really effective if it is done as part of a complete house insulation project. Replacement windows incorporating double glazing are available, but they are expensive and seldom worth the cost. Secondary double-glazing panels, which you can fit yourself, are much cheaper and are just as effective.

Loft conversions

To gain more space in your home you can extend it either upwards or outwards. The loft could be an ideal place for an extra room. The suitability of a loft for conversion is governed by two criteria: the shape of the roof and its method of construction. The shape determines how much space is convertible, usually the area in which you can stand upright. In most houses with sloping roof ends, only part of the roof space will be suitable for conversion. In terraced houses, however, or houses with gable ends, all the roof space can be used.

However, the most important factor determining whether or not a loft can be converted is the roof structure. Many modern houses have lightweight prefabricated roof supports, called trussed rafters, in which the weight of the roof is evenly distributed over all the members. Remove one strut and the roof may fall in. In older houses the rafters and struts were built up as part of the house and fairly heavy timbers were used, so it is possible to take out some of the supports to create space providing extra bracing is placed elsewhere. It is probable, too, that thicker joists will be needed for the floor of the room as the existing ceiling joists will not be adequate to support the extra weight of people and furniture.

Access to the loft may be by a fixed flight of stairs or a spiral staircase. If the hatchway is above a landing it will probably need to be resited, perhaps in a small bedroom. The main disadvantage of a spiral staircase is that it may be difficult or impossible to get large items of furniture into the loft. If the loft is to be used only occasionally, a pull-down ladder will suffice.

Obviously a loft conversion is outside the scope of the average DIY handyman. You should engage either a builder who specializes in loft conversions or one of the firms that advertise nationally. Planning permission is not required providing that you do not exceed the original height of the building, but Building Regulations must be met.

Extensions

If your loft is not suitable for conversion you can expand outwards by adding an extension. You will only need planning permission if the extension exceeds 70 cubic metres, or 15 per cent of the total house area up to a maximum of 115 cubic metres, providing again that the original height of the building is not exceeded. This does not apply, however, to a terraced house: for these the limit is 50 cubic metres or 10 per cent up to 115 cubic metres. No extension may be more than 4 metres high if it is within 2 metres of a boundary, and you may not cover more than 50 per cent of your ground area, not including the area of the house itself.

Planning permission will be needed if the extension is to extend beyond the front building line, except for a porch not covering more than 2 square metres, less than 3 metres above ground level and not less than 2 metres from a boundary fronting on to a highway.

A major extension, in excess of 70 cubic metres and providing extra habitable rooms, should preferably be brick-built and incorporated with the main structure of the house. It will require architect's plans and the work should be carried out by a qualified builder. Planning permission should be obtained before the work is started, and Building Regulations must be complied with, particularly regarding foundations and the insulation of walls. There may also be covenants to observe and a neighbour's 'right to light' to consider. If you have a mortgage, then permission may be required from the building society (or other loan source), and if the property is leasehold you will certainly have to obtain the landlord's approval.

The cost of such an extension can run into several thousands of pounds; to pay for it you may be able to obtain a second mortgage from your building society or a personal loan from the bank. Such an undertaking needs very careful consideration, not only with regard to the cost of construction but also the cost of heating and lighting and keeping the place maintained. Before embarking on such a project it is wise to explore fully all other possibilities; if extra rooms are the main requirement you may be able to achieve this by partitioning one large room to make two; if you want a more spacious living room, it may be possible to take out an internal wall and make one room out of two.

If, however, you decide that a major extension will be worth the cost, and the possible disruption of the household for several weeks, you could try one of the firms that offer 'package deal' extensions. The extensions are standard designs from which the customer can choose the one most suited to his needs and/or pocket and an all-inclusive price is quoted. That is fine if one of the designs is just what you are looking for, and 'package deal' schemes work out far cheaper than an extension built to your own specifications.

Unfortunately there are many so-called 'cowboy' firms who offer quick, attractively-priced work: quick because the work is done by inexperienced and non-qualified labourers intent only on collecting a wage packet, and cheap because inferior material is used. Often this type of work does not meet the Building Regulations requirements and has to be redone by a professional builder.

Avoid, therefore, anyone who is not a member of a recognized professional body (such as the Federation of Master Builders) unless you have seen evidence of their workmanship or they have been recommended by someone whose word you trust.

Engaging an architect

Obviously, if you are to spend a great deal of money on an extension you will want the best advice available. A good architect will, through his training and experience, be familiar with most aspects of building work, and will have the skill required to convert your ideas into workable plans.

Again, personal recommendation is the best way to find a good architect, otherwise the Royal Institute of British Architects (see Appendix) will supply you with names of members in your area who specialize in whatever type of work you want done.

Once you have found an architect you can, if you wish, let him handle the whole procedure from start to finish. He will draw up the designs and specifications needed for planning permission and Building Regulations approval. He will get estimates from builders and will make sure the work is up to standard once it has begun. You should, however, agree the costs at the very outset and should tell your architect just how much you can afford to spend. He will advise you within those limits.

The architect's fees are laid down in a standard scale by the RIBA's Condition of Engagement. The fee is usually a percentage of the total cost of the building and should be paid in instalments at each stage of the work. You can save part of the fee, however, by engaging an architect to supply drawings and do the rest yourself.

Finding a builder

If you decide on this course of action, you must first obtain planning permission, and then seek out your builder. Consider whether you want a builder who will do a complete job, or whether you want to engage the specialist tradesmen yourself, thereby employing 'direct labour'.

Most small builders have a full-time staff for only the 'wet trades' – bricklaying, plastering and concreting. For the other trades, such as electrical work, plumbing and decorating, he will sub-contract. You can ask the builder for an estimate for the complete job, including all trades, or you can ask for an estimate for the basic 'wet trades' and engage the sub-contractors yourself.

Employing direct labour can save costs, because you can buy fittings and finishes yourself at one of the many discount DIY shops. But you must let your architect know in advance that you intend to use this method as he will need to draw up separate sections for each sub-contractor.

Whether you go for a complete job or employ direct labour, approach at least three builders for estimates and let them know that they are in competition with others. Unless the work is a major undertaking it is often best to find a local man employing only two or three people. Many such firms offer skilled work at low cost.

Once you have found a builder whose estimate suits you, go through the specifications with him to establish exactly what the estimate will include. Then draw up a formal agreement, or get your solicitor to do it for you, and ask the builder to sign two copies. This now becomes a legal contract.

One of the hazards of employing a small builder is that such firms are very prone to bankruptcy when bank interest rates are high. If you make payments in arrears you should be able to avoid losing money, but if the builder does go bankrupt you will be faced with the problem of finding another one to complete the work. The National Home Enlargement Bureau (see Appendix) is in the process of launching a Bureau-bonded builder contract. Under this contract the NHEB guarantees to find another building firm to undertake the unfinished work.

Building Regulations

Any home improvement involving building work must conform to the Building Regulations; these were drawn up to protect health and safety and they cover such matters as construction materials; foundations; resistance of floors, walls and roofs to damp; fire precautions; insulation against heat loss and sound penetration; construction of stairways; ventilation; room sizes; drainage and the planning of lavatories.

The regulations sometimes stipulate certain standards without specifying how they are to be met. For example, cavity walls are *not* a requirement, they are merely a way of meeting the heat loss standard, known as the U value. In some modern houses this value is met, or exceeded, by timber-framing. For this, timber framework packed with insulating material is sandwiched between an outer brick wall and and an inner wall of insulation board.

Before work starts on your extension, therefore, you must obtain a form from your local building control office and return it filled in with details of the scheme, together with a set of drawings. It is an offence to commence work before providing this information. If the building control office is not satisfied with your proposals you may be told what you need to do to obtain approval, or you may have to submit a completely new set of details and drawings.

Scotland has its own Building Regulations which are similar to those in England except that the standards generally cover more aspects.

Modernizing a kitchen

Unless your house already has a fully-fitted kitchen, this is one area where you will probably want to make some improvements.

Modern kitchen furniture is built to standard metric measurements, and there are units designed to fit around a washing machine, dishwasher, refrigerator and cooker, and to take a sink unit and cooker hob. Floor-standing units measure 600 mm front to back and stand 800 mm to 900 mm high. Worktops are of various thicknesses, but 40 mm is best for a sturdy working surface. The units come in self-build packs with full instructions, requiring only a screwdriver and hammer to assemble.

Before you launch into converting your old-fashioned kitchen into a housewife's dream, make sure that everything will fit. Start by measuring the length and breadth of the room – in millimetres – so that you can work out how your units can be arranged. The chances of a row of units fitting exactly into the length of a wall are pretty slim, so you will have to decide where a gap should come and how to fill it. Be sure to allow space for doors to open (most units have doors that can be hung either left or right) and for drawers to be pulled out. When you have planned a run of floor units, select wall cupboards to fix above them that will cover the same length. This will give your kitchen a neat, symmetrical look.

You may find that you want to move the sink to fit in with your plan, but the position of the drain must be taken into consideration and you should seek the advice of a plumber. If you want to reposition a gas cooker, this will entail moving the gas point, which must be done by a gas board fitter, or by a gas board-approved contractor. Similarly, an electric cooker point should be moved or installed by a qualified electrician.

Do not overlook the question of ventilation if you want to avoid steamed-up windows and walls running with condensation. Plan for an extractor fan, fitted either in an outside wall or in a window, that is capable of making twelve to sixteen air changes per hour. An electrical dealer will be able to advise you on the size of fan required if you tell him the area of the kitchen in cubic feet. A cooker hood is also a worthwhile appliance for getting rid of cooking smells. There are two types of cooker hood: one changes the air, venting it to outside the house, the other recirculates the air through a special filter. Cooker hoods are not very effective over cookers with eye-level grills.

Good lighting will help you make the most of your kitchen. Fluorescent tubes provide an excellent and even illumination. Another possibility is to use spotlights, angled to illuminate worktops and the cooker hob. For extra light over work surfaces, fit concealed fluorescent tubes fitted under wall cupboards.

In older houses the kitchen is often cramped and tiny, but usually has a coal store and outside toilet attached. By knocking down the dividing walls the area of the coal store and toilet can be added to the kitchen, increasing its length by some eight feet or more. Removing the walls is a job for an expert, particularly as the one at the end of the kitchen will probably be load-bearing and will therefore require a lintel.

Alternatively the coal store and toilet area could be converted into one, with a door leading through from the kitchen, to make a utility room. If you keep the toilet as a toilet but provide it with an indoor entrance, there must be an intervening space. It is illegal to have a toilet that opens directly into a kitchen.

Improvement and repair grants

As well as grants for loft insulation there are also grants for certain home improvements and repairs. Local councils may give an improvement grant for work on houses which are basically sound and have an expected life of at least thirty years. The grant is a percentage of the total cost of the work, and varies from council to council. You can obtain details from the council offices or from the Citizens' Advice Bureau.

There is also an intermediate grant which is available for providing essential amenities such as sinks, toilets and bathrooms. The snag with this type of grant is that the council may insist on other improvements in addition to the ones you plan.

You can also obtain a repair grant for any property built

before 1919 needing substantial structural repairs to the walls, roof and foundations.

Repair grants and improvement grants are given at the local council's discretion, so your application will have a better chance of success if it is backed by an architect's plans and a surveyor's report.

Outside the house you are free to erect any outbuildings, such as a greenhouse, summerhouse, tool-shed, etc. You may also erect a garage, and providing it is more than 5 metres from the house it will not count as part of the planning permission allowance mentioned earlier. Once again, however, you cannot erect buildings that cover more than half the total ground area of the house. Self-assembly extensions are available that can be put up easily by a handyman and can be used as a conservatory or sun lounge. Providing no part of the extension is to be used as a habitable room, Building Regulations approval will not be required.

13 Moving on: the Second Home

'All right, if that doesn't bring us any results within a week we'll put it into the hands of an estate agent.'

Many people recognize from the start that their first home will be only a stepping stone, and will plan to move on within five to six years, during which time both their needs and their earning power are likely to have changed. During the time spent in the first home they will have learned how to deal with all aspects of running a home, both practical and financial, and of course the experience of acquiring their first home will prove useful when they come to move on.

Leaving a rented home

If your first home was rented and you have saved enough money while there to put down a deposit on a house, all the advantages of being a first-time buyer will apply to you, but you have obligations to your landlord that you must fulfil before moving out.

Naturally you will have to be up to date with your rental payments, but you must also give the landlord at least four weeks' notice in writing of your intention to leave. This applies to weekly, monthly or periodic tenancies. It does not apply, however, if you have a lease for a fixed period. In such cases, if you wish to leave before the period of the lease ends you must surrender the lease, which means handing back the property to the landlord and giving up all rights under the lease; alternatively, you can assign the lease, i.e. find someone to take it over. In the latter case the new tenant must be acceptable to the landlord. If the landlord has to find a new tenant, he may charge you rent for the time the property is empty.

You may also, by the terms of your contract, be liable for redecorating the house or flat and carrying out any necessary repairs before you leave. If you are assigning the lease it is quite possible that the new tenant will be willing to redecorate and carry out repairs, and a reasonable landlord will probably accept this arrangement.

Whether or not to sell

Selling a home can be a lengthy and expensive business, and no one should contemplate it lightly. Unless you are being forced to move by circumstances you should consider very seriously all other alternatives, particularly home improvements (as described in Chapter Twelve). The slogan 'Don't move - improve' adopted by the manufacturers of home improvement equipment is, as far as it goes, good advice. It is often cheaper to modernize or extend your home than to buy a new one. But you may, of course, have little choice, if your job takes you to a different area or some unforeseen change in your environment makes a move desirable.

One of the problems of buying and selling is that the market fluctuates - sometimes it is a sellers' market, sometimes a buyers', but seldom is it both. So you may find there are plenty of houses for sale but have difficulty in selling yours, or that you can sell your own house easily enough but can not find a suitable house to buy. Before you do anything about buying or selling, therefore, ask the advice of an estate agent or building society manager who will know the market trend.

Having the house valued

When you decide to sell, the first thing you will want to consider is how much to ask for the property. You may be able to get some idea by seeing how much is being asked for similar property in the area. But this can be very misleading. First, although you may have seen a nearby house advertised at a certain price, that does not mean that it actually fetched that amount.

Also, although the house may have appeared to be identical to yours, it may have had improvements made that you could not have seen, or it may have been generally in a better - or worse - condition.

Your best bet is to contact several estate agents, tell them you are thinking of selling your house and invite them to give you a valuation. You are under no obligation to engage any of them at this stage and the valuation should be free of charge. Make sure, however, that the agent visits your house - do not accept a valuation given over the phone.

Most of the valuations will probably be around the same figure, but if any are much higher or lower than the rest ignore them. If an estate agent quotes an obviously low price it means he is looking for a quick sale and is prepared to take a low commission; if he quotes a high price he is overpricing in order to get a high commission and is prepared to wait for it. In the first case you lose out financially, in the second case your house may be on the market for months before you find a buyer, and perhaps then only after lowering the price.

Selling through an estate agent

Engaging an estate agent to sell your house requires more care than buying through one, because there is a fee for selling. Competition between estate agents is fierce, and some will ask a smaller fee than others in order to get your business, but generally the charge is about 2 per cent of the sale price. Often it will be ½ per cent less if the agent handles the property exclusively. First of all, then, establish what the agent's fee will be and make sure you know exactly what it includes. It may not include advertising, for example, in which case you should specify how much you are willing to pay for advertisements and insist that he does not go above that amount without consulting you first. Find out the conditions of his agency. Some agents ask for the sole agency for a period, say, a month, which means that if you appoint another agent as well and he sells the house, you will still have to pay a fee to the first agent. Be even more wary of 'sole selling rights', because then the agent will charge a fee even if you sell the house yourself.

If you were well satisfied with the estate agent through whom you bought your present house, you might like to use him to sell it for you, or you can choose an agent by personal recommendation. Alternatively you should be safe enough with an agent who is a member of one of the professional bodies such as the Royal Institution of Chartered Surveyors or the Incorporated Society of Valuers and Auctioneers.

After advising you on a price the agent will, at your invitation, draw up particulars for prospective buyers and will note any special features, such as recently installed central heating, a garage, a modernized kitchen - all of which are good selling points. He will also take a photograph of the house to display in his window and have printed in advertisements.

The estate agent's first action will be to notify people on his books who are looking for property similar to yours, and you may be lucky enough to find a buyer within a few days. Failing that his next step will be to have leaflets printed and advertisements placed in the local press. Also, with your permission, he will place a 'For Sale' board outside the house.

Another service the agent provides, and it is an important one, is that he will vet all prospective buyers before putting them in touch with you. He will find out if they have arranged for a mortgage and will probably offer to help find them one if they have not, as many estate agents are also agents for building societies. Through careful questioning, the agent will decide whether the enquirer is a genuine buyer. Some people go on bogus house hunts just to nose round other people's homes and some of course do it for more sinister reasons, but the experienced agent can spot a phoney a mile off.

Once the agent has found a prospective buyer he will contact you to find out when it is convenient to view the property. He may accompany the buyer or not, but he will certainly do so if you have provided him with a key so that he can gain entry if you are not at home.

Many house vendors engage more than one estate agent, but it is debatable whether this is necessary, or advisable. Certainly there should be no need to do so for at least a month and there is no harm in giving the agent the sole agency for that period. He will work more quickly and efficiently if he knows that at the end of the month he may be faced with competition. In any case it is inadvisable to engage more than three or perhaps four agents since confusion can arise.

The contracts race

As mentioned in Chapter Six, it is becoming more and more common for vendors to ask for a preliminary deposit from a prospective buyer. And if more than one agent is used, and you have a string of interested enquirers, asking for a deposit from each of them will lead you headlong into a contracts race. Of course, you will not be the sufferer, financially, and you may even sell your house more quickly by deliberately provoking competition among buyers. But put yourself in their position: in a contracts race somebody loses – often more than one person – and may well finish up worse off by several hundred pounds if they lose out at a late stage in the negotiations; and even if you are negotiating with only one buyer, a preliminary deposit is an extra burden upon him at a time when he is faced with several necessary expenses. So do not ask for a deposit, which is in any case no guarantee that the prospective buyer will buy, and do not be the starter in a contracts race that will give you little satisfaction and will cause hardship to others.

Selling privately

You can, of course, save yourself some money by selling your house privately and thereby avoiding an estate agent's fee. Your main problem will be how to arrive at a fair asking price. There are three factors to consider: the price you paid for the house; how much property in the area has increased in value; and how much you have spent on improvements. One person who will be able to help you with the second factor is your building society manager, who will be aware of the local trend and can tell you by what percentage property values have risen. So, for example, if you paid £20,000 for your house five years ago, and prices have risen by 10 per cent in that time, your house should now be worth about £22,000 before you add on any extras for improvements. When you have arrived at a figure, add on about 5 per cent to give yourself scope for bargaining. You should also at this time decide whether to include such fittings as carpets and curtains. Your decision will be partly dictated by your carpeting and curtain needs in your next home, but if, as is most likely, they will not fit without alteration then leave them where they are. Carpets and curtains make a good selling point, and similarly you could consider including other major items such as a plumbed-in washing machine or a cooker.

The main disadvantage of not using an estate agent is that you will have to advertise the property yourself. Local evening and weekly papers are the best choice; you can also advertise in such magazines as *Dalton's Weekly*, *Homefinder*, *House finder* and *House Buyer*. Newspaper and magazine advertisements are expensive, so make the wording brief but attractive. Highlight the main selling points, but take care to be accurate: a buyer who can claim he was misled by your advertisement could claim damages under the Misrepresentation Act of 1967. If possible, give your phone number only, not the address, so that you will not be bothered by people calling unexpectedly. Have further details of the house written down and ready to hand for when someone phones, so that you can tell them more about the house and answer any questions.

How to word a newspaper advertisement

You can get some idea of how to word your advertisement, and how not to, by looking at the way other people have done it. For example:

For Sale. Freehold, detached bungalow. Elevated position. Well placed for shops and buses. Lounge, dining room, kitchen, three bedrooms, bathroom w.c. Gas-fired central heating. Garage. Large garden. Price required £25,000. For details phone ...

That advertisement tells people what they want to know, and also much of what they already know. If the advert is placed in the 'Houses for Sale' columns, then why say 'For Sale'? And there is no need to say that £25,000 is the 'price required': that is obvious. Nor is it necessary to say 'For details phone ...': the phone number itself is sufficient. So six words could have been saved in that advertisement without detracting from it in any way. You can also save wordage by using abbreviations, for example, w.c., c.h., r.v. (rateable value) and s.d. (semi-detached), but do not start making up your own: prospective buyers will not want to ring you just to find out what 'lfr' means, only to discover that it stands for 'large front room'.

DIY conveyancing

Once you have decided to sell your home you should inform your solicitor, unless you want to do your own conveyancing. DIY conveyancing can be risky for buyers, especially first-time buyers, but the risks are fewer for vendors, particularly if details of the property being sold are registered at the Land Registry.

You are not involved with searches, and if any complications do arise they will be the buyer's problem, not yours. However, when you sell your house you will presumably be buying another, and may not want to do your own conveyancing on that. There seems to be little point in doing your own conveyancing on the house you are selling and engaging a solicitor for the house you are buying. But if you want to give it a go, there are two books which will help enormously; one is *The Conveyancing Fraud* by Michael Joseph, who is himself a solicitor, and the other is *The Legal Side of Buying a House* published by the Consumers' Association. Both can be ordered from bookshops.

Alternatively you could go to one of the conveyancing organizations, which claim to be cheaper than solicitors. Since anyone can set up a conveyancing firm, regardless of qualifications or experience, it is best to choose one recommended by the National Association of Conveyancers.

Showing prospective buyers your property

If you are wise you will have prepared your house for the visits of prospective buyers before putting it on the market – making sure any outstanding painting and decorating jobs have been done, getting the garden straight and generally make sure that the house is clean and tidy. Do not do too much, though. You will not impress anyone by re-papering all the rooms: more likely the prospective buyers will wonder what is underneath, and in any case their taste in wallpaper is likely to be different from yours.

Your best approach is to give your visitors a quick guided tour of the house and then withdraw for a while so that they can wander about at will. Later you should sit down and discuss any points they may wish to raise (see Chapter Four), and eventually discuss the price. Do not be disappointed if your visitors express great interest but do not make an offer: they may want to ponder over it longer, or they may prefer to make the offer through the estate agent, especially if it is lower than your asking price. They will know, of course, that you are asking more than you expect to get – the 5 per cent you added – and you will know that they know, and so on, but that is what bargaining is all about.

Accepting an offer

If your prospective buyers make an offer through the estate agent, the agent may advise you as to whether to accept it or not; he will know from experience whether the offer is genuine and the buyers are likely to go through with it. But if he advises you to take the offer, and it is lower than your asking price, give yourself time to think about it. Perhaps you can do a little bargaining yourself, like meeting the buyers halfway on their lower offer in return for your carrying out a few repairs or improvements. Do not let the estate agent rush or bully you. Catherine and Chris, remember, had the price of the house they bought reduced, and had the roof repaired as well. They would have been happy just to get the price down and pay for the roof themselves, but the house had been on the estate agent's books for some time and he was anxious to get rid of it, so he persuaded the vendor to accept Chris and Catherine's offer.

Once you have settled on a price, the process of conveyancing can begin. First you must instruct your solicitor: he will want to know the name and address of the buyers, and of their solicitor, and the agreed price. He will also want to know if you have come to any arrangement with the buyers about fittings. If you have any doubts about what fixtures you can remove, such as shelving or wall-hung cupboards, he will be able to advise you. But you must let the buyers know of your intentions as they may consider that they have bought the house as they first saw it. Even if they agree to your taking down a wall-hung cupboard, they will not be pleased if half the wall comes down with it.

Remember that, as when buying a house, you should tell your solicitor everything he needs to know, so that he will not have to phone you or write to you. He will, at an early stage, decide a completion date suitable to both you and the buyers. On that day the buyers hand over the money, and the house is no longer yours. You must move out. The solicitor will also make arrangements for you to pay off the mortgage on the property you are selling (his charge for this is standard: £30).

Selling property in Scotland

It was explained in Chapter Six that the procedure for buying a house in Scotland differs somewhat from the English method; so, too, does the procedure for selling. There are estate agents in Scotland, but most sales are still made through solicitors, who handle the whole transaction from start to finish, with separate charges for each stage. First the solicitor will act as agent: preparing particulars of the house, advising the vendor what price to ask, advertising in newspapers and at the local Solicitors' Property Centre, dealing with offers and negotiating the price.

The charge for this part of his service will not exceed 1½ per cent of the price. This includes adjusting and closing the binding contract.

Then the solicitor will deal with the conveyancing, in much the same way as an English solicitor. The charge for this is on a sliding scale recommended by the Law Society of Scotland and based on the price of the property. The scale is £100 for the first £5,000 of the price and then £10 per £1,000 up to £40,000, and £5 per £1,000 thereafter. To give an example, a house sold for £25,000 would have a maximum commission on sale of £375 and the scale fee would be £300. In addition the solicitor can charge for postage and phone calls and newspaper advertisements. He may also handle your repayment of the loan on the house, or discharge of the mortgage (his charge for which will be £30).

14 Moving out

Reproduced by kind permission of *Ideal Home* magazine

When you moved into your first home, all you had to worry about was shifting your personal belongings and perhaps a few pieces of furniture stores in readiness, and having new furniture and fitments delivered at the right time. Probably a few car or van trips were enough to transport everything to your new home.

But that was probably a few years ago, and by now you will have a fully-furnished home and a stock of clothes, bedding, crockery, kitchen equipment, ornaments and a host of other items to be packed and moved to home number two. And that is before you begin to think about all that stuff in the attic, the garage and the garden shed. Your first reaction to the move is likely to be panic – followed quickly by the reflection that perhaps you should call the whole thing off. But it is too late now: contracts have been exchanged and on completion day you must move, or alternatively, if you are a tenant, you will have informed your landlord of your intentions and he will have a new tenant waiting to move in.

But at least you have the exciting prospect of your new home to spur you on, and if you plan the move well ahead and prepare for it methodically this major upheaval can be minimized.

The first thing you must consider is whether to engage a removal firm or to do the job yourself. Most removal firms will do everything needed, including packing crockery and ornaments, dismantling bedsteads, taking down mirrors, taking up carpets and lino and providing special packing for fragile items such as hi-fi equipment and TV sets. You will, of course, be expected to strip beds and pack your clothes, and pack food into boxes. But you could, at that point, and for a price, go and stay with friends, or at an hotel, and let the removal men get on with it. Having the packing done for you will increase the removal bill by about one-third, and even a local move involving only one journey can be very expensive – up to £300 on average for the contents of a medium-sized semi-detached house. The extra cost might be worthwhile, however, for self-employed people who would lose money by taking time off to pack.

Finding a removal firm

If you decide to let a removal firm do all the work for you, choose one that is a member of the British Association of Removers. The BAR sets high standards for its members and has a consumer affairs department to investigate complaints. But if you are tempted to have the move carried out cheaply by one of the many 'cowboy' firms you will have no redress if furniture is damaged and crockery broken. Moving furniture and fragile goods requires a little more than just brawn and muscle and it is far better to trust it to experts.

Unless you have only a small amount to move, perhaps the contents of a small flat, it is best to avoid the temptation of doing your own removal, for several reasons. First, there is the cost of hiring a van and the cost of the petrol: remember that if you have to make several journeys between the two homes in a small van the costs will rise steeply, particularly if you are paying a mileage charge. And at the end of each of those journeys there will be another session of loading or unloading, possibly up and down stairs. You must decide for yourself if the cost in terms of sheer exhaustion makes any possible saving worth while, but if you are still keen to have a go here are a couple of tips: shop around for a hire van and use the largest vehicle you think you can handle; ask the rental company the capacity of the van (the average house needs about 800 cubic feet), and work out from that how many trips you will have to make. But remember that you will achieve only about 75 per cent of the van's capacity when you load it.

Furniture removal is a highly competitive business, so it pays to shop around if you are going to have the job done professionally. The cost of the move will depend on the amount to be moved, the distance and the day; weekday moves are generally cheaper than Saturdays and holiday periods. Plan your move as far in advance as possible and obtain estimates from at least three firms, but first decide what you are going to take and what you will leave behind. The removal firm will send an estimator to give you a quote, and part of his job is to decide what size van is needed. So if an extra trip has to be made because you either overlooked something or had a change of mind, there will be an extra charge which could be heavy.

Fixtures and fittings

In deciding what to take you are controlled to some extent by the law. You cannot take fixtures, which roughly interpreted means anything that is permanently attached to the house such as the central heating system and built-in furniture. Nor can you take a greenhouse, shed or garage if it is built on foundations. Even trees and large shrubs are classified as fixtures, and so is the garden soil, despite the case of the keen gardener who actually took his lawn.

If you do take a fixture, the new owner can take you to court, especially if it was a selling point, as in the case of the man who replaced a beautiful ornate front door with a cheap one. The new owner sued him and the door was put back.

Fittings are easily-removable items such as light-bulbs and lampshades, plug-in appliances and free-standing kitchen units, and these you can take. But the distinction between fixtures and fittings is poorly defined and for some items, such as bookshelves, fixed wall-mirrors, curtain-rails and towel-rails, the only way to solve the problem is to come to an amicable agreement, in advance, with the new owner.

Removal estimates

When the estimator calls, go round the house with him and make sure he understands what is to go and what is to stay. Draw his attention to any items that will need special care, such as antiques, pendulum clocks and fragile pieces of furniture. If you have a piano, ask if the removal men are experienced in handling this type of instrument. Some say they are but prove not to be. If the instrument is valuable, if it is a grand, or if stairs are involved at either end of the journey, you would be well advised to have it moved separately by a specialist piano removal firm.

Do not forget to show the estimator items which may be outside the house, such as garden furniture, tools, the lawnmower and garage contents.

Finally, ask him if the quote will include transit insurance, and if so what it will cover. Most large companies offer insurance cover at about 5 per cent of the removal charge. Alternatively you should be able to obtain a temporary extension to your home contents insurance to cover the move: check the small print, either way, or you could be unlucky enough to discover, too late, that for example the policy excludes scratching and denting of furniture - precisely the sort of damage that is likely to occur when goods are in transit.

The removal company's insurance will almost certainly have a clause excluding jewellery, furs and valuable collections of, for example, stamps or coins. You will find, too, that compensation is paid at the market value, so do not buy new furniture or equipment before you move unless you intend to have it delivered direct to your new home by the dealer.

A fixed charge is usually made for removals; once you have accepted and signed the quotation it becomes a contract and the terms cannot be altered except by the special provisions stated. Check these before signing and consider whether they are fair and reasonable. Lastly, check that the removal time and date are correct.

Packing

Start your packing in the last week or two before the move, and begin with a ruthless clear-out of the loft, cupboards and garden shed and anywhere else where junk has accumulated over the years. You may be able to sell a few unwanted items, which will help defray the removal costs, and consign the rest to the dustbin or council tip.

For packing, collect strong cardboard boxes (apple boxes from a greengrocer are ideal). You can buy tea-chests for about £1 each, or the removal firm may loan them free of charge. Use the tea-chests for packing glass and china, double-wrapped in newspaper. Plastic dustbin liners are useful for packing linen, bedding and curtains. Clothes and other lightweight items can stay in their drawers, but do not lock the drawers as they may have to be removed for transit. Clear out bottles and other containers from make-up drawers, the bathroom cabinet and the medicine chest. Make sure the tops are firmly fixed and pack in small boxes. Put first-aid equipment in a separate box and keep it handy in case of emergency.

To pack pot-plants make a metal-foil tray and place it in the bottom of a cardboard box. Water the plants daily before the move and put them in the box on the day of the move. Small garden plants should be wrapped in plastic sheeting together with a clod of earth and stood upright in a cardboard box.

Try to set one room aside as a packing and storage area. Do not pack too many heavy items in one box: the removal men will not thank you for it and you may have to move the boxes yourself when it comes to unpacking. Books are particularly heavy and should be distributed evenly in medium-sized boxes; if you put them in tea-chests, do not fill the containers over half-full. Where possible, pack hi-fi equipment, radios, video-recorders, cassette-players and the like in their original boxes, or try to obtain replacement boxes from a dealer. If you are taking carpets, have them lifted by experts before the move takes place, and arrange for them to be re-laid in your new home.

Run down the contents of the refrigerator and freezer and defrost as near to removal day as is convenient. The freezer can be kept in continuous use if you are moving only a short distance (the contents will keep without thawing for up to eight hours). Ask for it to be loaded last and taken off first so that it can be reconnected quickly. It is also a good idea to make the cooker a 'last on/first off' item. If you have a gas cooker, make sure to arrange for it to be connected the day you arrive. The gas company will want at least one week's notice.

Before moving day, draw up a plan of your new home and number the rooms. Then mark on the plan the position for each piece of furniture. Label the furniture with the appropriate room number so that the removers know exactly where it must go. As an additional guide, make up numbered cards which can be attached to the door of each room.

Moving day

Try to get a good night's rest before removal day, and in the morning have a substantial breakfast: it may be your last good meal for several hours. You can help the move considerably by having all drawers containing heavy or fragile items removed and placed on the floor next to the piece of furniture to which they belong. You should also attach 'Do not remove' labels to any items which you will require on your journey, such as coats, handbag, small cases, etc.

If you have pets, remember that they cannot be carried in the van. Cats, small dogs and puppies can be transported in special cartons available from a pet-shop; on no account let them run loose while the furniture is being removed. Cage birds can be kept in their cages, preferably covered, or, for the journey only, in a shoe-box perforated with airholes. Goldfish can be carried in a plastic bag containing ten times as much air as water.

If you have tropical fish, the water must be maintained at the correct temperature during the journey. The best way to do this is to use large vacuum storage jars, sealed except for an airhole, which will keep the temperature even for about eight hours.

When the removers arrive it will help if you have just made a pot of tea. Removal men thrive on tea, but do not offer to lace it with something to keep the cold out on a winter's day!

Keep the pot well topped up throughout the move, and do not get impatient if the men stop for a break now and then – they may be big strong lads, but they are also human.

Your move will go much more smoothly if someone can travel ahead of the van to open up the new home in readiness, and perhaps to ensure that the van will be able to park outside. Opening up the house will give it a chance to air before the furniture arrives. Before the van arrives the rooms-plan should be fixed where the removers can refer to it easily, and someone should also stand by the entrance to direct operations and advise of any last-minute changes to the rooms-plan.

At the old home, have a final check to see that everything has been loaded before the van moves off: it is your responsibility to ensure that nothing is left behind. Then go round the house and shut all the windows; turn off the water at the rising main, and turn off gas and electricity at the meters.

Do not forget to arrange for the house keys to be handed over to the new owner, estate agent or caretaker, as the case may be. Finally, make sure the van driver knows where he is going, and how to get there. Tell him of any parking or access problems that he may encounter. If there are any parking restrictions outside the house you should notify the removal firm well in advance so that they can arrange for police co-operation.

As soon as possible after the move, have a thorough check of the condition of your goods. If there are any claims for damage or breakages, make them within seven days of the move.

Now the weeks of preparation and waiting are over, and you can look forward to the excitement of setting up your second home – which is pretty much where we came in!

15 If Disaster Strikes Your Home

This, the shortest chapter in the book, deals with the unpleasant subject of what happens should you be faced with the dreadful but nevertheless very real possibility of being made homeless. Every year thousands of people lose their homes – through fire, flood or some other catastrophe – and find their lives shattered and their world turned upside down. In a matter of minutes the bedrock of their security has gone, leaving them helpless, frightened and bewildered.

What happens if you lose your home

However careful you are to ensure the safety of your home, there is still the chance of a disaster happening, caused perhaps by factors beyond your control. And however well you have insured your property, that is small comfort at the moment disaster strikes and you have lost most, or all, of your possessions. Eventually, of course, the house will be rebuilt and the contents replaced, but that will not happen for many weeks or months. So where do you live in the meantime? And how can you acquire quickly such essentials as food, clothing, furniture and even money?

Your rights in law

Fortunately the Housing (Homeless Persons) Act of 1977 takes care of the first problem. The Act was designed to ensure that no one should be homeless 'as a result of any emergency such as flood, fire or other disaster'. It makes all local authorities responsible for the immediate rehousing of disaster victims regardless of their age, financial standing or size of family.

How quickly you would be rehoused depends largely on the size of the town in which you live. Most large towns and cities have a department which specializes in dealing with homeless persons and can act quickly in an emergency; in smaller towns and rural districts accommodation may not be readily available but the local authority may ask for assistance from a neighbouring council. All London boroughs may call on the GLC for help.

Initial accommodation may be in a hostel or reception centre, but as soon as possible a homeless person or family will be moved into a council house or flat. Once there, they will be treated as ordinary tenants and may stay as long as they need providing they are prepared to pay the normal rent. They do not, however, become 'secure tenants' as defined by the 1980 Housing Act.

Who will help provide essentials

It is comforting to know that no one need fear being left without a roof over his head, but the local authorities' obligation stops there. The Act does not provide for the replacement of furniture, clothes, bedding and other essentials that may have been lost. Many councils will provide whatever help they can, and if children and elderly or infirm people are involved a supplementary benefit may be claimed from the Social Security office to help with immediate cash needs. Practical help is also available from various voluntary services.

The Women's Royal Voluntary Service is one of the major organizations that gives help to the homeless. Working in close collaboration with local welfare departments, the WRVS is always on call to provide food, clothing and bedding. The Salvation Army is another nationwide organization willing to help, particularly with furniture.

In addition to these national organizations there are many local charitable bodies which can help in all manner of ways. The police, fire service and welfare officers who are experienced in dealing with distraught families bereft of their homes will contact all possible sources of help. And the services of the Citizens' Advice Bureau are always there to help and guide people in need.

It should be stressed that alternative accommodation under the Homeless Persons Act is provided only if the dwelling is completely uninhabitable, or if the building is deemed to be unsafe. Local authorities are loath to give up accommodation needed by people on their waiting list, and if at all possible they will carry out temporary repairs to make the disaster-stricken house inhabitable. The cost of such repairs can be claimed on the building insurance.

Appendix

British Association of Removers
279 Gray's Inn Road, London WC1X 8SY
Tel. 01-837 3088
Will supply information about members in your area.

British Chemical Dampcourse Association
51 High Street, Broom, Bidford on Avon, Warks.
Tel. Bidford on Avon (0789) 772716
Will investigate complaints against members.

British Insurance Association
Aldermary House, Queen Street, London EC4N 1TU
Tel. 01-248 4477
Publishes many useful leaflets on all aspects of insurance, including a table showing how to estimate rebuilding costs.

British Wood Preserving Association
150 Southampton Row, London WC1B 5AL
Tel. 01-837 8217
Provides advice on preserving woodwork against dry rot, woodworm, etc. and will supply names of firms which will carry out free inspections.

Building Centre
26 Store Street, London WC1E 7BT
Tel. 01-637 9001
A good place for ideas on home improvements; exhibits include bathrooms, kitchens, heating systems and building materials; there is a well-stocked bookshop and a library of trade directories and manufacturers' catalogues.

Building Societies' Association
14 Park Street, London W1Y 4AL
Tel. 01-629 0515
Will supply list of members.

Consumers' Association
14 Buckingham Street, London WC2N 6DS
Tel. 01-839 1222
The consumers' watchdog. Publishers of *Which?*, *Money Which?* and *Handyman Which?*, etc.

Corporation of Mortgage and Finance Brokers
24 Broad Street, Wokingham, Berks. RG11 1AB
Tel. Wokingham (0734) 785672
Will supply names of mortgage brokers in your area.

Federation of Master Builders
33 John Street, London WC1N 2BB
Tel. 01-242 7583
Also regional branches in Birmingham, Bristol, Cambridge, Cardiff, Leeds, Newcastle, Sevenoaks and Southport.

Federation of Private Residents' Associations
83 Cambridge Street, London SW1
Tel. 01-834 8921
An advisory body for residents' associations.

Heating and Ventilating Contractors' Association
34 Palace Court, London W2 4JG
Tel. 01-229 2488
Will supply names of your local specialist in these fields.

Housing Corporation
149 Tottenham Court Road, London W1P 0BN
Tel. 01-387 9466
A government-backed organization which provides loans for self-build projects and assists co-ownership and shared ownership schemes. Among its several publications is a booklet listing all co-ownership associations and the number of units they hold. A manual on self-build houses is also available.

Incorporated Association of Architects and Surveyors
Jubilee House, Billing Brook Road, Weston Favell, Northampton NN3 4NW
Tel. Northampton (0604) 40412

(Her Majesty's) Land Registry
Lincoln's Inn Fields, London WC2A 3PH
Tel. 01-405 3488
All property in England and Wales must be registered with this government body.

Law Society
113 Chancery Lane, London WC2A 1PL
Tel. 01-242 1222
The professional organization for all solicitors in England and Wales.

Law Society of Scotland
PO Box 75, 26 Drumsheugh Gardens, Edinburgh EH3 7YR
Tel. 031-226 7411
A useful leaflet issued by this organization for solicitors in Scotland is *Buying or Selling a House*, which details the scale of charges.

Loft Conversion Advisory Bureau
594 Kingston Road, London SW10

Mobile Homes Residents' Association Ltd
163 Wood Street, Walthamstow, E17
Tel. 01-520 2261
Deals with the interests of residents of mobile homes other than caravans.

National Association of Citizens' Advice Bureaux
110 Drury Lane, London WC2
Tel. 01-836 9231
Will tell you where you can find your nearest Citizens' Advice Bureau.

National Association of Conveyancers
2-4 Chichester Rents, London WC2A 1EJ
Tel. 01-549 3636
If you are looking for cut-price conveyancing, this association will provide a list of its members, who must abide by its rules.

National Association of Estate Agents
21 Jury Street, Warwick CV34 4EH
Tel. 0926 496800
This association lays down a code of conduct for members.

National Cavity Insulation Association
178-202 Great Portland Street, London W1N 6AZ
Tel. 01-637 7481
Members must work to a minimum standard laid down by the association, and anyone wishing to have cavity insulation is strongly advised to use only contractors approved by the NCIA. A free leaflet and names of members in your area are available.

National Federation of Building Trades Employers
82 Cavendish Street, London W1
Tel. 01-637 4771

National Federation of Housing Associations
86 Strand, London WC2E 7HE
Tel. 01-240 2771
Deals with the formation and conduct of housing societies and associations.

National Federation of Roofing Contractors
15 Soho Square, London W1V 5FB
Tel. 01-439 1753
Will supply names of members in your area.

National House-Building Council
58 Portland Place, London W1
Tel. 01-637 1248

National Home Enlargement Bureau
PO Box 67, High Wycombe, Bucks. HP15 6XP
Tel. High Wycombe (0494) 711649
Advisory service for house-owners wishing to enlarge their homes.

National Home Improvement Council
26 Store Street, London WC1E 7BT
Tel. 01-637 9709
Works in conjunction with the Building Centre (q.v.) at the same address.

National Inspection Council for Electrical Installation Contracting
237 Kennington Lane, London SE11 5QS
Tel. 01-582 7746
Will supply a list of approved electrical contractors.

National Supervisory Council for Intruder Alarms
St Ives Road, Maidenhead, Berks.
Tel. Maidenhead (0628) 37512
Maintains a register of approved installers who will fit alarms to British Standards, acceptable to insurance companies and the police.

Office of Fair Trading
Field House, Breams Buildings London EC4R 1PR
Tel. 01-242 2858
A statutory body which administers the Consumer Credit Act and looks after consumer interests. Will deal with all types of consumer complaints.

Royal Incorporation of Architects in Scotland
15 Rutland Square, Edinburgh EH1 2BE
Tel. 031-229 7205
Professional organization for Scottish architects.

Royal Institute of British Architects
66 Portland Place, London, W1N 4AD
Tel. 01-580 5533
Runs advisory service which will put you in touch with an architect suitable for the work you require.

Royal Institution of Chartered Surveyors
12 Great George Street, London SW1P 3AD
Tel. 01-222 7000
The professional association for surveyors and estate agents.

Royal Society for the Prevention of Accidents
Cannon House, Priory Queensway, Birmingham B4 6BS
Tel. 021-233 2461
Provides advice on all aspects of safety. Publishes *Care in the Home* and has many free leaflets and booklets on home safety.

Society of Solicitors in the Supreme Courts of Scotland
2 Abercromby Place, Edinburgh EH3 6JZ
Tel. 031-556 4070
The professional organization for Scottish solicitors.

Scottish Building Contractors Association
13 Woodside Crescent, Glasgow G3 7UP
Tel. 041-332 7144

Scottish Federation of Housing Associations Ltd
56 Hanover Street, Edinburgh EH2 2DX
Tel. 031-226 6810
Promotes voluntary housing organizations in Scotland.

Solid Fuel Advisory Service
Hobart House, Grosvenor Place, London SW1
Tel. 01-235 2020

Index

Accidents in the home, 82, 88-91
   electrical, 89-90
   falls, 88-9
   first aid, 90-91
APR (Annual Percentage Rate of Total Charge for Credit), 106-7
Architect, engaging an, 118-19

Bailiffs and sheriffs, right of entry of, 95-6
Banks:
   budget accounts, 104-5
   direct debiting, 105-6, 107
   loans from, 107
   mortgages, 28, 29
   standing orders, 105, 107
Bargaining, 47
Bathrooms, 6
Bedrooms, 3-4
   children's, 4
'Bogus callers', 88
British Association of Removers, 135, 144
British Chemical Damp-courses Association, 62, 144
British Insurance Association, 75, 76, 78, 144
British Standards Kitemark, 87
British Wood Preserving Association, 62, 144
Budget accounts:
   bank, 104-5
   stores and supermarkets, 106
Budget payment scheme, 104
Builder, finding a, 119-20
Building Centre, 144
Building Cost Information Service, 76
Building Regulations, 120-21, 123
Building societies, 23
   mortgage guarantee policy, 73-4
   mortgages, 23-6, 29, 61
   savings accounts, 23
   valuation survey fee, 61
Building Societies' Association, 145
Bullion glass, risk of fire from, 84-5
Bungalows, 3, 9

Burglar alarms, 87-8
Burglars, 82
  how to deal with, 97-8
  making home secure against, 86-7
Bus services, 31
Buying a home:
  choosing where to live, 30-32
  conveyancing, 56-61, 64-7
  estate agents, 32-4
  Homeloan scheme, 62
  insurance, 73-80
  matching property to loan, 29-30
  mortgages, 22-9
  moving in, 68-72
  recently-built houses, 49-55
  structural survey of house, 62-4
  see also conveyancing, house-hunting

Car servicing, 72
Caravans, 60
Central heating systems, 44, 112-13
  electrical 'warm-air' system, 112
  floor and ceiling systems, 112
  thermostats for, 114
  'wet' system, 112
Certificated Bailiffs, 96
Change-of-address, notifying, 71-2
Chimneystacks, 38
Circuit-breakers, 83
Citizens' Advice Bureau, 19, 121, 142, 146
The Commission for New Towns, 15
Condensation, 42
Conservation areas, 47-8
Consumer Credit Act, 107
Consumers' Association, 131, 145
Contract, signing the, 59-60
Contracts race, 64-5, 128-9
Conveyancing, 56-57
  completion, 65
  contract and covenants, 59-60
  contracts race, 64-5 128-9
  cut-price, 65-6
  DIY, 130-31
  local authority and land registry 'search', 60, 66
  preliminary deposit, 58
  in Scotland, 66-7
  solicitors' fees, 60-61, 65
The Conveyancing Fraud (Joseph), 131
Cooker hoods, 121-2
Co-ownership schemes, 19-20
Corporation of Mortgage and Finance Brokers, 145
Council houses, 3, 16
Council officials' right to enter private homes, 93
Covenants, 60
Credit cards, 106
Credit sale agreement, 106
Credit schemes, 106-7
Crime Prevention Officer, 87
Customs and Excise

officials, right of entry
by, 94

Damp and condensation,
  39-40, 42
Damp-proof course (DPC),
  40
Decorating materials,
  inflammable, 85
Deferred Payment
  Mortgage Scheme, 28
Detached houses, 2-3, 7
Development Board for
  Rural Wales, 15
Dining room, 6
Direct debiting, 105-6
Distraint, 96
Doctor and dentist, finding
  new, 72
Double glazing, 115-16
Downpipes, 38-9
Drainage systems, 39
Driving licence, notifying
  change of address on,
  71-2
Dry rot, 40-41, 62

Electric cooker, 70
Electricaire, 112
Electricity, electrical:
  accidents, 89-90
  connecting, 70
  fires, 82-3
  heating, 112, 113-14
  paying bills, 104
  reading meter, 70
  rewiring, 83
  tariffs, 109-10
  wiring circuits, 43
Electricity Board officials:
  inspection by, 63

right of entry by, 93-4
Employee-tenants, 19
Endowments politicies/
  mortgages, 25-6
  low-cost, 25-6
  non-profit, 25
  with-profit, 25
Entertaining guests in
  rented accommodation,
  18
Estate agents, 45, 46
  buying house through,
  32-4
  selling house through,
  127-8
Extensions, building,
  117-18
  Building Regulations,
  120-21
  engaging an architect,
  118-19
  finding a builder, 119-20
  'package deal', 118
  planning permission,
  117, 119
  self-assembly, 123
Extractor fans, 121

Falls in the home, 88-9
Family Practitioners'
  Committee, 72
Federation of Master
  Builders, 145
Fire in the home, 82-6
  bullion glass, 84-5
  electrical, 82-3
  inflammable decorating
  materials, 85
  inflammable furniture, 85
  kitchen, 83-4
  smoke detectors, 88

153

tackling, 86
Fire extinguishers, 85
Fireplace, bricked-up,
 ventilation of, 38
Fire Protection Association, 84
First aid, 90-91
Fixtures and fittings, 37, 136-7
Flats, 9
 converted, 9
 maisonettes, 3, 10
 purpose-built, 3, 9
Freehold property, 33
Furnished accommodation, 16, 18
Furniture:
 inflammable, 84-5
 inventory of, 18
 removal, 134-5

Garages, 6
Gardens, 6-7
 erecting outbuildings in, 123
Gas:
 central heating, 112, 113
 connecting appliances, 70
 paying bills, 104
 reading meter, 70
 tariffs, 107-9
Gas Board officials, right of entry by, 93-4
Grants, local authority:
 home improvements and repairs, 16, 121, 122-3
 intermediate, 121
 loft insulation, 115
Guttering, 38-9

Heating, heaters:
 central heating, 44, 112-13
 convector heater, 114
 electric fires, 114
 insulating pipes, 114
 radiant fire, 114
 storage heaters, 112 113-14
Hiring a van, 69-70
Hire-purchase agreements, 106
Holiday, burglary precautions while on, 87
Home:
 insulating, 114-15
 improving, 111-23
 mobile, 11-12
 losing your home, 141-3
 moving out, 134-40
 renting, 14-21
 safety in the, 82-91
 selling, 125-33
 types of, 2-3, 7-13
 see also buying a house
Home Improvement Grants, 16, 121, 122-3
Homeloan scheme, 62
Homelessness through natural disasters, 141-3
Hot-water system, 44, 113, 114
Household expenses, 100-110
 bank loans, 107
 budgeting for bills, 104-5
 central heating, 112-13
 credit schemes, 106-7
 direct debiting, 105-6
 electricity tariffs, 109-10
 extensions, 117

154

gas tariffs, 107-9
rates, 101-4
solid fuel and oil prices, 110
House-hunting, 35-48
   bargaining, 47
   conservation areas, 47-8
first visit and assessment of house, 36-8
   inspection of property, 38-45
   making an offer, 45
   vacant possession, 46-7
   House Purchaser's Agreement, 49, 52
   value of, 54-5
Houses:
   bungalows, 3, 9
   council, 3
   detached, 2-3, 7
   new, 10-11, 49-55
   self-build, 12
   semi-detached, 2-3, 7-8
   terraced ('town'), 8, 11
   with vacant possession, 46-7
Housing Act (1980), 15-16, 20, 142
Housing and Planning Acts, 93
Housing associations and societies, 19, 20-21
Housing Corporation, 19, 20, 21, 145
Housing (Homeless Persons) Act (1977), 141, 143

Improvements to the home, 111-23
   Building Regulations, 120-21
   central heating, 112-13
   double glazing, 115-16
   engaging an architect, 118-19
   extensions, 117-18
   finding a builder, 119-20
   improvement grants, 122-3
   insulation, 114-15
   loft conversions, 116
   modernizing a kitchen, 121-2
   outbuildings, erecting, 123
   repair grants, 122-3
   storage heaters, 113-14
Incorporated Society of Valuers and Auctioneers, 127
Institution of Electrical Engineers, 89
Insulation, 114-15
Insurance, 73-80
   assessing value of contents, 77-8
   buildings, 74-5
   combined buildings and contents, 77
   contents, 76-7
   estimating rebuilding costs, 75-6
   index-linked, 75
   tenants, 78-9
Insurance companies, loans from, 28-9
Interest rates, 27
Inventory of furniture, 18

Kitchen(s), 5-6
   fires, 83-4
   lighting, 122

modern designs, 5
modernizing, 121-2
renovating, 6, 120-21
ventilation, 122
Kitchen units, 121-2
  gallery assembly, 5
  L-shaped,
  single-line, 5
  U-shaped, 5

Landlord (of rented accommodation):
  agreeing fair rent with, 17
  agreement of, 17-18
Land Registry, 61, 146
Lands Tribunal, 103
Law Society, 65, 66, 146
Leasehold property, 33
The Legal Side of Buying a House, 131
Lighting circuits, electrical, 43
  junction-box, 43
  loop-in, 43
Local council/authority:
  home imrovement grants, 121
  insulation grants, 115
  loans, 28, 62
  mortgages, 28
  rehousing of homeless people by, 131-2
Local authority accommodation, *see* Council houses
Locks and bolts, 86-7
  deadlock, 86-7
  hinge locks, 87
  mortise deadlock, 87
  mortised bolts, 87
  padlocks, 87

window, 87
Loft:
  conversions, 116
  insulation, 115

Mail, redirection of, 71
Maisonettes, 3, 10
Master Builders' Federation, 76
Meter-reading, 70, 93
Misrepresentation Act (1967), 130
'Missive of sale' (in Scotland), 67
Mobile homes, 11-12
Mortgages, 22-9
  bank, 29, 117
  building society, 23, 30, 61, 117
  deferred payment schemes, 28
  endowment, 25-6, 29
  insurance company, 28-9
  local authority, 28
  repayment, 25, 26-7
  tax relief on, 27-8
  terms of, 24-5
  types of, 25
Mortgage guarantee policy, 24, 73-4
Moving in, 68-72
  connecting supplies, 70-71
  finding doctor and dentist, 72
  hiring a van, 69-70
  preparing the house, 69
  redirecting mail, 71-2
Moving out, 134-40
  finding removal firm, 135-6

fixtures and fittings, 136-7
moving day, 139-40
packing, 138-9
removal estimates, 137
Multi-way adaptors, danger of, 82-3

National Association of Conveyancers, 66, 131, 147
National Cavity Insulation Association, 115
National Federation of Housing Associations, 12, 21, 147
National House-Building Council ((NHBC), 11, 50-52, 147
  Conciliation Office, 53
  Handbook, 50
  House Purchaser's Agreement (10-year guarantee), 49-50, 63
  making claims to, 52-3
  value of the guarantee, 54
National Home Enlargement Bureau, 120
National Television Licence Records Office, 105
Neighbours' rights, 97
New/recently-built houses, 10-11
  buying, 49-55
New Town Development Corporation, 15
Newspaper advertisements, 34, 130
NICEC (National Inspection Council for Electrical Contracting), 43, 148

Office of Fair Trading, 148
Official Secrets Act, 94
Oil:
  central heating, 112-13
  price of, 110
Option accounts, 106
Option Mortgage Scheme, 26, 28
Outbuildings, erecting, 123

Packing, 138-9
Parking facilities, 31
Pets, moving, 139
Pipe lagging material, 114
Planning permission, 60, 116, 117, 118, 119
Plastics materials, inflammability of, 84
Plumbing systems, 43-5
Police, rights of the, 92, 94-5
Polystyrene, inflammability of, 84, 85
Post Office engineers, right of entry, 94
Public Health acts, 93

Radiators, 44, 112, 113
Rates, rateable value, 101
  assessment of, 101-2
  obtaining a reduction, 102-4
  paying, 102
  revaluation, 96, 112
Rebuilding costs, 74-5
  estimating, 75-6
Rehousing homeless people, 141-2, 143
Removal firms, 135-6
  estimates if, 137
Remuneration Certificate, 65

Rent, agreeing a fair, 17
Rent Acts, 19
Renting a home, 14–21
  agreeing a fair rent, 17
  co-ownership schemes, 19–20
  furnished and unfurnished accommodation, 16–17
  giving notice, 125
  a home with a job, 19
  landlord's agreement, 17–18
  moving out, 125
  Rent Acts, 19
  shared ownership schemes, 20–21
  shorthold tenancy, 17
  surrendering or assigning lease, 125
  'Tenants' Charter', *see* Housing Act (1980)
Rising damp, 39–40, 42, 62
Roof, roofing:
  faults, 38–9, 47
  insulation of, 114–15
  trussed rafters, 116
Royal Institute of British Architects, 118, 119, 148
Royal Institution of Chartered Surveyors, 127, 148
Royal Society for the Prevention of Accidents, 91, 149

Safe as Houses? (ROSPA), 91
Safety in the home, 82–91
  accidents, 88–91
  burglaries, 86–8
  fires, 82–6
  locks and bolts, 86–7
Salvation Army, 142
Sasine Register, Edinburgh, 67
Scotland:
  Building Regulations, 120
  conveyancing, 66–7, 133
  selling property, 133
Self-build group, 12
Self-build houses, 12
Selling your home, 125–33
  accepting an offer, 132
  advertising property in newspapers, 129–30
  contracts race, 128–9
  DIY conveyancing, 130–31
  having the house valued, 126–7
  privately, 129–30
  in Scotland, 133
  showing property to prospective buyers, 131–2
  through an estate agent, 127–8
Semi-detached houses, 2–3, 7–8
Settlement of buildings, 41–2
Shared ownership, 20–21
Shorthold tenancy, 17
Sitting/living rooms, 4–5
Smoke detectors, 88
Solicitors, conveyancing, 56–61
  fees, 60–61, 65
  role and functions, 57–60, 64–5
  Scottish, 133

Solicitors' Property Centre,
  66, 133
Solid fuel:
  central heating, 112
  price of, 110
Solid Fuel Advisory
  Service, 110, 114
'Staircasing', 20
Stamp Duty, 30, 61
Storage heaters, 112, 113-14
  damper-controlled, 113
  fan-assisted, 113
  static, 113
  storage fan, 113-14
Survey of house, structural,
  62-4

Tax relief, 27-8
Telephone:
  reconnecting or installing,
  70-71
  saving stamps for paying
  bills, 106
Tenants, tenancy:
  agreeing fair rent, 17
  co-ownership
    schemes,
    19-20
  employee-tenants, 19
  housing authority, 16
  insurance for, 78-9
  landlord's agreement,
    17-18
  'right to buy' of, 16, 20
  secure, 15-16
  shorthold agreements, 17
'Tenants' Charter', see
  Housing Act (1980)
Terraced houses ('town
  houses'), 8, 11, 12-13
Thermal jackets, 114

'Town houses', 11
Trespassers, 93
  how to deal with, 97-8
TV detector-van engineers,
  right of entry of, 94
TV licence, saving stamps
  for, 105

Underpinning of
  foundations, 42
Unfurnished
  accommodation, 16

Vacant possession, 46-7
Valuation Officers of
  Inland Revenue,
  right of entry of, 96-7
Vehicle Licensing Centre,
  Swansea, 71
Ventilation, 121
Visitors' and tradesmen's
  rights, 98-9

Walls, penetration of damp
  through, 39-40
Warrant for Delivery, 95
Warrant for Possession, 95
Water authorities personnel,
  right of entry of, 94
Water supplies, connecting,
  70
Wet rot, 41, 62
Window locks, 87
Wiring circuits, electrical, 43
  lighting, 43
  radial, 43
  ring-main, 43
Women's Royal Voluntary
  Service, 142
Woodworm, 42, 62
Writ of Assistance, 94